Cherubim

MW00958204

Exploring the Extradimensional Hypothesis

Extradimensional Vehicles, Ancient Nephilim Technology,

and Interstellar Prophecies Revealed!

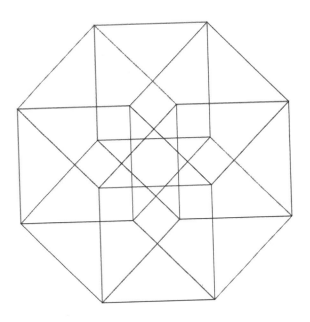

Josh Peck

Author of *Quantum Creation*

Cherubim Chariots

Exploring the Extradimensional Hypothesis

Extradimensional Vehicles, Ancient Nephilim Technology, and Interstellar Prophecies Revealed!

ISBN-10: 1507878877

ISBN-13: 978-1507878873

Table of Contents

TABLE OF CONTENTS

Table of Figures

Acknowledgements

This book is dedicated to my loving wife Christina, my two children Jaklynn and Nathan, and my brother Cody.

I have a lot of people to thank for this book. First and foremost I thank my Lord and Savior, Jesus Christ. I also want to thank my wonderful family: my wife, children, and brother. Outside of the Peck home, I have many people who have been there for us and the ministry in various ways. For more reasons than I can count, I'd like to thank S. Douglas Woodward, Mark Flynn, Perelandra Kilns, Derek and Sharon Gilbert, Gonz Shimura, Basil, John and Pam Haller, Doug Krieger, Jim Wilhelmsen, Cris Putnam, Dr. Michael Lake, Dr. Michael Heiser, Ray Gano, Dan Duval, Natalina, Brian Godawa, Peter Goodgame, David Lowe, Parker J. Cole, Chris White, Dr. Ken Johnson, Shoshana Reynolds, and the many, many others who have supported us, encouraged us, and kept us in prayer.

Foreword

Written by Mark A. Flynn

www.markaflynn.com

The information suddenly and freely available to the public because of the Internet allowed for progress toward a greater discernment of the UFO phenomenon. Gradually the perception of UFO and encounter researchers as being eccentric or worse, delusional, has waned. Today the study of the phenomenon has become more common and UFO related terms have become a part of popular culture.

Those who describe themselves as UFO believers generally fall into two categories. The first group elucidates that the appearance of UFOs and human interaction with the "beings" that control them occurs because our planet is being visited by aliens from outside our solar system and has been for thousands of years.

The second group would theorize that the beings are not extra-terrestrial, but *extra* or *intra-dimensional* entities. These beings do not originate from outside our solar system but have always been near us (as far as this is understandable in the intra-dimensional sense) since the beginning of human creation. Some in this group would describe the visitors as angelic.

If true, the second category begs further questions. Who created the non-human entities that seem to exist outside of our perception and why? Are the beings restrained somehow from freely inhabiting the human realm? Are there laws that must be followed in order to communicate with us and us with them? Finally, (and this is discussed in *Cherubim Chariots*) what is the physical nature of angelic beings and the realm that they inhabit?

From a Judeo-Christian worldview, the statements listed below are fundamental in continuing this discussion from the position that the UFO phenomenon is likely intra-dimensional. They establish a starting foundation, just as a description of the function of an integrated circuit would first require a basic knowledge of electricity, circuit design and Boolean logic.

1. God exists.

2. God created the universe but is not restricted to it.

3. God created angelic beings.

4. God created human beings.

FOREWORD

While some people today would not accept these statements as axiomatic as I do, they lead us to a position where we can identify the "visitors" and understand that they have been interacting with men since the entities described as "Watchers" first came down from their realm to earth at Mount Hermon. (David Flynn's *Watcher Website* was the first on the Internet to explore these questions and provide answers in the light of the Old Testament.)

Human, angelic/alien interaction continues today and not necessarily in the manner of man being a merely passive *visitee*. It appears likely that human beings can initiate contact by helping to create *passageways* from the angelic (or demonic) realm into ours. An example of a purposeful effort to accomplish this occurred in the late 1940s.

Described as a charismatic genius, as well as an eccentric mystic, Jack Whiteside Parsons endeavored to create a passageway or window into our world in 1946. He was a key founder of the Jet Propulsion Laboratory in Pasadena, California. The inventor of Hitler's V-2 "revenge weapon" and leader of the Operation Paperclip rocket development team, Wernher von Braun, referred to him as the "father of modern rocketry." As a boy Parsons studied classical literature, later becoming interested in esotericism through his reading of *The Golden Bough*, by the Scottish anthropologist, Sir James George Frazer. Destined to become a talented chemical engineer and inventor, he was expelled from a military academy for blowing up toilets and claimed to have successfully invoked Satan to appear to him at the age of 13.

Parsons became a member of the Aleister Crowley headed, Ordo Templi Orientis (OTO), in 1941 and joined the California based branch, known as The Church of Thelema. (Crowley defined Thelema as: "The science and art of causing change to occur in conformity with will.") Crowley, also known as the "Great Beast" or "Frater Perdurabo", admired Parsons' alchemic skill and dedication to the god Pan so much that he considered him to be the most valued member in all of the order. While practicing magic rituals as the head of the church of Thelema, Parsons acquired a mansion in South Pasadena that he developed into a bohemian commune, and welcomed any "exotic types" to join. The commune later became known as the "Parsonage."

Stepping aside a bit from all of the Parsons-Hubbard-Crowley history, I often think of Montana when considering the question of the nature of the UFO phenomenon. There is also a surreptitious link between Montana, my home town of Helena, and Jack Parsons. Malmstrom air force base near Great Falls was a hotspot of UFO activity during the 1970s while my brothers and I were growing up in the nearby town of Helena. The late Dr. Jesse Marcel Jr. practiced as an ear, nose, and throat specialist there. He and our father discussed his experience viewing artifacts from a crashed UFO as a young boy in Roswell, New Mexico, which was where we first heard of the Roswell incident from our Dad sometime in the late 70s. This occurred well before knowledge of the event became mainstream after Philip J. Corso's and Stanton T. Friedman's work. The founder of Scientology, Lafayette Ronald Hubbard, also grew up in Helena. Besides creating his own religion, Hubbard, a Science fiction writer and U.S. Navy officer, moved into the Parsonage around 1945 where he and Parsons eventually became close friends. Parsons was impressed with Hubbard and thought he was the most Thelemic person he had ever met, and mentioned this to his mentor, Crowley.

Through his association with Crowley and work in the OTO, Parsons came to believe in the reality of magic (spelled "magick" according to Crowley) as a force that could be explained through quantum physics. He believed that he could bring about the incarnation of a Thelemite goddess that he called "Babalon" onto Earth by altering the constraints of normal space-time through his will via the practice of Thelema.

Parsons called the magical operation he was planning the "Babalon Working", and allowed Hubbard to take part in it as his documenting "scribe", since he believed Hubbard to be exceptionally perceptive at detecting magical phenomena. Both

Parsons and Hubbard believed in Thelema magic so completely that they went out into the Mojave Desert and performed the Babalon working, which was nothing less than a specific effort to "punch a hole" between realms. The final ritual took place in January 1946.

Jack Parson believed, as did Van Braun, L. Ron Hubbard, and Aleister Crowley, that powerful non-human entities existed, but in a realm somehow separate from man. Although there seemed to be a prohibition on the type and quantity of interaction allowed, that prohibition could be altered by man's activity on earth. It is worth recognizing that the Roswell event occurred one year after the Thelemic ritual in the Mojave Desert, as well as a huge increase in UFO sightings that continue to this day. The story of L. Ron Hubbard and Jack Parsons' Babalon Working illustrates that the nature of the UFO phenomenon is more profound than the majority living today realize.

Apart from the understanding provided from research concerning the identity of the Watchers and their reasons for interacting with humanity, exploration into the specific nature of their realm and their physical makeup has not been as thoroughly studied. So the questions remain, what is the nature of the realm and why does it continue to be so separate and invisible? Will this present condition between "their" and our realm ever change? Josh Peck explores some of these issues in *Cherubim Chariots.*

FOREWORD

Finally, it must be mentioned especially in the light of the topic of this book, that one true measure of a person's love of God is interest in His word, His nature and His creation, both seen and unseen. What truly loving relationship exists where each member is not interested in knowing as much as possible about the other?

Luke 11:9 "And I say unto you, Ask, and it shall be given you; seek, and ye shall find; knock, and it shall be opened unto you."

Mark A. Flynn

January 16, 2015

Introduction

There are two prevailing theories to explain the sightings of unidentified flying objects and nonhuman entities. One states they are of a physical origin (usually extraterrestrial) and one states they are extradimensional (what some might call "spiritual"). The more popular of these two is the Extraterrestrial Hypothesis (ETH). This is a common view that is promulgated through our culture in the form of the media, entertainment, and even some of our religious belief systems.

The lesser known view is the Extradimensional Hypothesis (EDH), which can sometimes be confused with the Interdimensional Hypothesis (IDH).[1] Wikipedia defines the IDH as such:

The interdimensional hypothesis (IDH or IH), is an idea advanced by Ufologists such as Jacques Vallée that says unidentified flying objects (UFOs) and related events involve visitations from other

---

[1] Throughout this book, I will be referring to this theory as the EDH or extradimensional hypothesis. For reasons I detail in my book *Quantum Creation: Does the Supernatural Lurk in the Fourth Dimension?* I believe this to be the more correct and informative term for what we will be dealing with in this book.

"realities" or "dimensions" that coexist separately alongside our own. It is an alternative to the extraterrestrial hypothesis (ETH).[2]

The difference is that "interdimensional" seems to denote capability while "extradimensional" denotes origin. For example, if we as humans were to discover a way to travel between dimensions, we could be considered an interdimensional species, or beings with interdimensional capabilities. If an entity originates from a higher dimension than our own, it would be considered an extradimensional being. The EDH we will be looking at throughout this book states UFOs and their pilots, at least some of them, originate from a higher dimension than the three of space in which we currently reside.[3]

What the EDH view has working against it is the fact that it almost always leads to a discussion of religious/spiritual beliefs, many of which differ greatly from one another. Many times, the view of an extradimensional existence is translated into the definition of spiritual existence. This is fine and good for the spiritually-minded, but what of those who subscribe to a different belief system, or no belief system at all? What if we were to take our views of a spiritual existence and translate them back into

---

[2] http://en.wikipedia.org/wiki/Interdimensional_hypothesis
[3] For more information on this, check out this article written by author and researcher Cris Putnam - http://newswithviews.com/Putnam/cris103.htm

extradimensional terms? What we would find is the two go hand-in-hand more than what we might originally think.

For quite a long time now, the ETH has dominated the interpretation of UFOs and other alien phenomena. I propose we give equal effort and scrutiny to the EDH and see how it fits. To only consider one view is comparable to wearing only one shoe; one foot will be comfortable but eventually the other will be left dragging behind. It would be far more beneficial to wear both shoes, walk around, and see which one fits better. For too long the world has been wearing only one shoe. It's old and tattered, but it is familiar and comfortable enough. What if the world were to try putting a new shoe on the neglected foot? We might just find that this new shoe, though suspected to be uncomfortable by its outward appearance, actually fits better than the old one. Sure, it is different and may require some time to break in, but how else will we know which we prefer unless we try both on and walk around for a while?

Throughout this book, we will get into topics that are usually found resting in the fringe of serious discussions about UFOs, religion, and science. That is not to assume these topics have no merit. Yes, we will look at a fair amount of speculation, however we will explore the solid foundation those speculations are built upon.

We will look at the strange creatures called "cherubim" and explore the possibility of their extradimensional origins. We will see how such creatures have had an influence over ancient history and culture. We will also look at ancient reports of flying craft to see if we can find clues showing their extradimensional nature. After that, we will dive into the strange world of ancient technology as well as the offspring of extradimensional beings and humans.

We will take a deep look into scripture written by ancient prophets, such as Ezekiel and Zechariah, to see if they were describing extradimensional beings and craft entering our realm. We will also explore possible modern-day signs in the topography of the planet that may point to extradimensional visitations in antiquity. After that, we will look to the stars in conjunction with scripture to see where all of this is leading in our near future. Lastly, we will see what this all has to do with the human race; personally and as a whole.

As always, my hope is not only to inform you, but to provoke further study and research on your own. There is a wealth of information out there; far more than can be included in a book such as this. I hope to broaden your horizons and cause you to consider a new perspective. Most of all, I hope to lead you to the truth. At the very least, I hope to convince you to search for the truth yourself, exploring all possibilities, and not necessarily sticking with the one that benefits you the most on a personal basis, but boldly accepting the one that is most correct and genuine, even if it means you must sacrifice your current paradigm.

Thank you for reading, take care, and God bless!

Josh Peck

www.MinistudyMinistry.com

joshpeckdisclosure@gmail.com

Who Are the Cherubim?

Purpose vs. Appearance

In our physical world of three spatial dimensions, we tend to classify things by their outward appearance. We sort things out in accordance to size, shape, color, and a variety of other physical attributes. This method works out great for objects that are physical, as we understand physicality; however this does not seem to work quite as well with things outside of our three dimensions of space.

The cherubim are true extradimensional entities. They vary in appearance, yet they are known as cherubim based on their purpose; their reason for existence. The job of the cherubim seems to be protection in various forms. We see this aspect in the religious beliefs and myths of various cultures.

Descriptions of the cherubim's appearance varies depending on culture, time period, and who is providing the description. The common thread, as far as appearance, is they all seem to be an amalgamation of various types of animal and human forms. This aspect of the cherubim is repeated throughout all accounts, though the specifics seem to vary.

The Garden of Eternity

The first mention we see of cherubim in Jewish Scripture is found in the book of Genesis. After Adam and Eve had rebelled, God expelled them from the Garden of Eden. After that, He placed cherubim in the garden to protect the Tree of Life.

"So he drove out the man; and he placed at the east of the garden of Eden Cherubims, and a flaming sword which turned every way, to keep the way of the tree of life."

Genesis 3:24

An interesting thing to note which might describe an attribute of the Garden of Eden can be found when we consider the word "east". In the original text, the word "east" comes from the

Hebrew word *qedem* and has a double meaning.[4] Most times, it simply means east. On the surface, this seems to be the appropriate translation. However, *qedem* can also mean ancient, aforetime, earliest time, and beginning, among others.[5]

The word *qedem* is used to describe an attribute of God in other places of Scripture.

"The eternal God is thy refuge, and underneath are the everlasting arms: and he shall thrust out the enemy from before thee; and shall say, Destroy them."

Deuteronomy 33:27

In this verse, the word "eternal" was translated from the Hebrew word *qedem*. This shows the timeless attribute of God. Describing God as eternal conveys the idea that He is outside of time itself; He has no beginning or end.

This may help explain an aspect of creation that is not commonly considered. Earlier in the book of Genesis, we read about the attributes of the Garden of Eden:

---

[4] "Hebrew Lexicon :: H6924 (KJV)." Blue Letter Bible. Accessed 19 Oct, 2014. http://www.blueletterbible.org/lang/Lexicon/Lexicon.cfm?Strongs=H6924&t=KJV

[5] This realization was first brought to my attention by Brenton Sawin of *Mysteries to Search.*

"And the LORD God planted a garden eastward in Eden; and there he put the man whom he had formed."

Genesis 2:8

The word "planted" comes from the Hebrew word *nata`* and also means "established".[6] Since the word "eastward" comes from *qedem*, this could be conveying the idea that the garden itself was originally established in a place outside of time as we know it. The fact that the garden had a beginning disqualifies it from being truly eternal, but this could be showing that it originated from a state outside the normal flow of time. This could be an attempt to describe a place of a different space-time than what we are familiar with. The Garden of Eden may have originated from a higher dimension.

If this is true, this could help explain further why Adam and Eve were expelled from the garden. There is a theory that states before Adam and Eve fell, they had access to all dimensions of created space-time. At the time of the rebellion, a split in the dimensions occurred. Adam and Eve were left "fallen" to the three dimensions of space and one of time that we are currently familiar with and the rest of the higher dimensions became inaccessible. Perhaps this was the purpose of the fruit of the Tree of Life.

---

[6] "Hebrew Lexicon :: H5193 (KJV)." Blue Letter Bible. Accessed 19 Oct, 2014. http://www.blueletterbible.org/lang/Lexicon/Lexicon.cfm?Strongs=H5193&t =KJV

CHAPTER 1

Before the fall, Adam and Eve were free to eat of any tree except for the Tree of the Knowledge of Good and Evil (Genesis 2:16-17). This means they were free to eat from the Tree of Life since it was already present in the garden (Genesis 2:9). If the fruit from the Tree of Life was there to sustain their state in eternity, we can begin to understand why Adam and Eve were denied access after they fell. Adam was told that if he were to eat of the Tree of the Knowledge of Good and Evil, he would surely die (Genesis 2:17). If Adam and Eve were to eat the fruit from the Tree of Life after they fell, they would have been in an eternal state of death. They would have been comparable to the unredeemable Serpent who first tempted them into rebellion. They would have had no chance of redemption.

After all of this, Genesis 3:24 tells us that cherubim guarded the garden along with *"a flaming sword which turned every way, to keep the way of the tree of life."* Note that the text does not necessarily imply the cherubim were handling the sword. The text only states that one was placed there. The turning every way aspect seem to come directly from the sword itself and does not seem to be caused by the cherubim.

It seems whatever this sword actually was, its purpose was to make it impossible for Adam and Eve to enter the garden again and have access to the Tree of Life. This sword may have been what was used to cause the split in dimensions of space-time. It was not until after Adam and Eve were driven out of the garden that this sword was set in place. If true, this would help explain why the Garden of Eden has never been found. It exists in a state that we no longer have access to. It is contained in a dimension higher than our own. It could very well be that the garden is still here on Earth. However, due to our limited perception, we could walk right through it and never know it. To this day, it's possible the sword and the cherubim are still performing their duty, thus the garden remains inaccessible.

The Ark and the Temple

Although we do not get much of a visual description of the cherubim in Genesis, we begin to get more details as we move forward through Jewish Scriptures. In the book of Exodus, we find the exact depiction of the Ark of the Covenant: the place where God would descend and fellowship with mankind. Atop the Ark of the Covenant were two cherubim made of gold. The construction of the ark and the cherubim are detailed for us in Scripture.

[18] And thou shalt make two cherubims of gold, of beaten work shalt thou make them, in the two ends of the mercy seat.

CHAPTER 1

¹⁹ And make one cherub on the one end, and the other cherub on the other end: even of the mercy seat shall ye make the cherubims on the two ends thereof.

²⁰ And the cherubims shall stretch forth their wings on high, covering the mercy seat with their wings, and their faces shall look one to another; toward the mercy seat shall the faces of the cherubims be.

²¹ And thou shalt put the mercy seat above upon the ark; and in the ark thou shalt put the testimony that I shall give thee.

²² And there I will meet with thee, and I will commune with thee from above the mercy seat, from between the two cherubims which are upon the ark of the testimony, of all things which I will give thee in commandment unto the children of Israel.

Exodus 25:18-22

From the text above, we learn that the cherubim have wings and faces (Figure 1). We also get a similar detail when the temple is described in the book of 1 Kings.

²³ And within the oracle he made two cherubims of olive tree, each ten cubits high.

²⁴ And five cubits was the one wing of the cherub, and five cubits the other wing of the cherub: from the uttermost part of the one wing unto the uttermost part of the other were ten cubits.

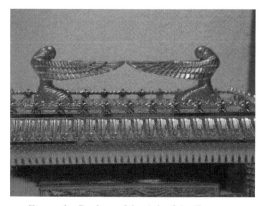

Figure 1 - Replica of the Ark of the Covenant

²⁵ And the other cherub was ten cubits: both the cherubims were of one measure and one size.

²⁶ The height of the one cherub was ten cubits, and so was it of the other cherub.

²⁷ And he set the cherubims within the inner house: and they stretched forth the wings of the cherubims, so that the wing of the one touched the one wall, and the wing of the other cherub touched the other wall; and their wings touched one another in the midst of the house.

²⁸ And he overlaid the cherubims with gold.

1 Kings 6:23-28

The Jewish historian Josephus stated that, based on the available descriptions of the temple, no one can know or even guess the true form the cherubim took.

"He also dedicated for the most secret place, whose breadth was twenty cubits, and length the same, two cherubims of solid gold; the height of each of them was five cubits they had each of them two wings stretched out as far as five cubits; wherefore Solomon set them up not far from each other, that with one wing they might

touch the southern wall of the secret place, and with another the northern: their other wings, which joined to each other, were a covering to the ark, which was set between them; but nobody can tell, or even conjecture, what was the shape of these cherubims. "[7]

We find even more detailed visual descriptions of cherubim in other ancient texts such as the book of Ezekiel. However, we are going to go into great detail concerning these passages later in this book. What we have looked at thus far will provide a framework we can build upon later.

Lamassu and Shedu

The Lamassu is the Assyrian equivalent to the cherubim. It was considered a protective deity that had the winged body of a lion or a bull with a human head. The Lamassu is portrayed as a female deity in writing.[8] The male counterpart to the Lamassu is known as the *"Shedu"* (Figure 2), though these are depicted less frequently.[9] The amalgamation of animals and human along with the protective nature of the creature shows a clear connection between the Lamassu and the cherubim of Jewish Scripture.

---

[7] Flavius Josephus *Antiquities of the Jews Book VIII* - 3:3
[8] Paul-Alain Beaulieu *The Pantheon of Uruk during the Neo-Babylonian Period*
[9] Jeremy Black and Anthony Green *An Illustrated dictionary, Gods, Demons and Symbols of Ancient Mesopotamia* The British Museum Press 2003

In the British museum, an excavated Lamassu can be found on display (Figure 3). This comes from northern Iraq, specifically from the palace of the king

Figure 2- Shedu Relief from Nimrud in the Vorderasiatisches Museum in Berlin

Ashurnasirpal II, who ruled between 883 and 859 B.C. in ancient Assyria. During his reign, Ashurnasirpal II turned the once-

provincial town of Nimrud, ancient Kalhu into the capital city. In the city, the palace of Ashurnasirpal II is described in many of the reliefs that contained what is known as the Standard Inscription. This inscription is important because it tells of the purpose of the Lamassu. The inscription states:

Figure 3- Lamassu from Nimrud in the British Museum

"I built thereon [a palace with] halls of cedar, cypress, juniper, boxwood, teak, terebinth, and tamarisk [?] as my royal dwelling and for the enduring leisure life of my lordship. Beasts of the mountains and the seas, which I had fashioned out of white

limestone and alabaster, I had set up in its gates. I made it [the palace] fittingly imposing. "[10]

It is said that the *beasts of the mountains and the seas* were the Lamassu themselves as they were sculpted from limestone. The purpose of these beasts was to guard, protect, and support important doorways in Assyrian palaces. The sculptor gave the Lamassu five legs so that from the front it would appear to be standing firmly while from the side it would appear to be striding forward.[11]

Pillars and Numbers

In his book *Forbidden Secrets of the Labyrinth: The Awakened Ones, the Hidden Destiny of America, and the Day After Tomorrow*, author and biblical researcher Mark A. Flynn puts forth a very interesting idea concerning the meaning of pillars in architecture. To quote Mark Flynn:

"A wedge or obstruction was set in place at the time when the union of God and men, heaven and earth, was interrupted. An appropriate illustration of this new state would be the symbol of the pillars. The most rigid and graceful of architectural edifices were set in place after Eden and now symbolically separate

---

[10] The Metropolitan Museum of Art (http://www.metmuseum.org/toah/works-of-art/32.143.2)
[11] Ibid.

heaven from earth. They were partly removed at the reconciliation between God and man that occurred through the death and resurrection of Jesus Christ. Pillars that represent the physical separation of heaven and earth still exist. "[12]

If this interpretation of pillars is correct, then we see a possible connection when we look at the meanings of certain numbers.

E.W. Bullinger did extensive research into the meanings of numbers found in the Bible. Though the entire body of text he put together is an interesting read, for our purposes here we only need to examine three of those numbers. According to Bullinger, the number 2 signifies division, 4 signifies creation (specifically material and physical, such as the earth), and 6 is described below:

"Six is either 4 plus 2, i.e., man's world (4) with man's enmity to God (2) brought in: or it is 5 plus 1, the grace of God made of none effect by man's addition to it, or perversion, or corruption of it: or it is 7 minus 1, i.e., man's coming short of spiritual perfection. In any case, therefore, it has to do with man; it is the number of imperfection; the human number; the number of MAN as destitute of God, without God, without Christ. "[13]

---

[12] *Forbidden Secrets of the Labyrinth: The Awakened Ones, the Hidden Destiny of America, and the Day After Tomorrow* by Mark A. Flynn, Defender, page 25
[13] *Its Supernatural Design and Spiritual Significance* by E.W. Bullinger – this can be read for free at http://philologos.org/__eb-nis/.

CHAPTER 1

When we consider the meanings of the pillars and numbers in reference to the Lamassu, we can make a possible connection.

If we think of the legs of the Lamassu as sets of pillars, we find that there are a total of 5 sets in the legs alone (including combining the fifth leg of each to make one set). As we learned earlier, the Lamassu and Shedu were used on either side of the palace doors to support a set of pillars. Including this set, we come to a total of six sets of pillars found within these cherubim-like creatures (Figure 4). This shows the division of Heaven and Earth (2 + 4) due to man's defiance toward God (6). This ties back to the original purpose of the cherubim in the Garden of Eden. Though this may be speculative, it supports the idea that other ancient cultures understood the purpose and importance of the cherubim.

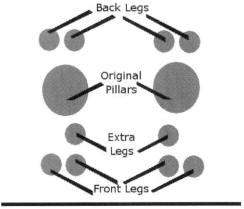

2 sets of Back Legs + 2 sets of Front legs + 1 set of Extra Legs + 1 set of Original Pillars = 6 sets of Pillars

Figure 4 - Bird's Eye View of sets of Pillars in the Lamassu and Shedu

Interpreting the Similarities

The main reason given for the similarities found in these creatures is ancient writers and sculptors borrowed ideas from neighboring cultures. This is a possibility, however this does not explain the vast differences in deities, beliefs, and religious practices that have been documented. Most notably, the Hebrew people of ancient Israel believed in one true Creator God whereas the neighboring cultures had more pantheistic beliefs.

Though not a popular theory, the possibility that ancient cultures actually witnessed these things firsthand could also explain the similarities. When considering the possibility of dimensions higher than our own, it is entirely possible that ancient cultures had encounters with extradimensional beings. This is what many of them had reported in their writings, such as in the books of Genesis and Ezekiel. If we take them at their word, humanity has been visited in the past by beings outside our current understanding of reality. This begs the question, and one we will take a closer look at later in this book, are these encounters still occurring today?

Extradimensional Entities of Ancient India

The Mahabharata

The Mahabharata is an ancient Sanskrit epic concerning the history of India. In its estimated 1.8 million words, the Mahabharata is perhaps most noted for the details it contains about the Kurukshetra War. We can find descriptions of chariots, both terrestrial and celestial (or perhaps *extradimensional*); in other words, of men and gods.

The Pushpaka

In the Mahabharata, we find a description of a chariot called the *Pushpaka*. The Sanskrit word *puspaka* (from *Pushpaka*) has a variety of meanings. From the Monier-Williams Sanskrit-English Dictionary:

Puspaka:

> *1. m. a kind of serpent*
>
> *2. m. N. of a mountain*
>
> *3. n. (rarely m.) N. of the self-moving aerial car of Kubera (also -vimAna n. ; it was carried off by the demon RAvaNa and constantly used by him till he was slain by RAma-candra, who then employed the car to transport himself and SItA back to AyodhyA)*[14]

There are other definitions as well, but these three are more than enough to suit our purposes here.

In the texts, we learn of the Pushpaka's ability for air travel:

---

[14]   Monier-Williams   Sanskrit-English   Dictionary: v0.3   RC1   -
http://lexica.indica-et-buddhica.org/dict/lexica

CHAPTER 2

"And he rode on that beautiful and sky-ranging chariot called the Pushpaka that was capable of going everywhere at the will of the rider."[15]

We also learn of the origins of the Pushpaka:

"And the lord of treasures sat on that excellent seat, the elegant Pushpaka, constructed by Viswakarma, painted with diverse colours."[16]

The interesting thing is that Viswakarma (sometimes written as *Vishvakarman)* is the deity of craftsmen and architects. In essense, he can be considered as the god of technology, but in the Vedas he is also seen as the ultimate creative force (later developed as Brahman).[17] He is sometimes referred to as the "Principal Architect of the Universe".[18, 19]

Another interesting description is found in the Mahabharata concerning the Pushpaka:

---

[15] The Mahabharata of Krishna-Dwaipayana Vyasa, Volume 1 Books 1, 2 and 3 (Kindle Locations 23611-23612). . Kindle Edition.
[16] The Mahabharata of Krishna-Dwaipayana Vyasa, Volume 1 Books 1, 2 and 3 (Kindle Locations 18520-18521). . Kindle Edition.
[17] http://en.wikipedia.org/wiki/Vishvakarman
[18] Ibid.
[19] This is especially interesting when we consider the nearly identical terminology used within Freemasonry.

"And the son of Raghu then, having worshiped that Pushpaka chariot, joyfully gave it back unto Vaisravana."[20]

We learn that the Pushpaka was something that was considered as worthy of worship. Not only was the god Viswakarma considered a deity, but also was his creation of the Pushpaka airship.

There is a common tradition that teaches the Serpent of the Garden of Eden was the one responsible for the development of ancient and modern technology. This view stems from certain verses in the third chapter of the book of Genesis:

[17] And unto Adam he said, Because thou hast hearkened unto the voice of thy wife, and hast eaten of the tree, of which I commanded thee, saying, Thou shalt not eat of it: cursed is the ground for thy sake; in sorrow shalt thou eat of it all the days of thy life;

[18] Thorns also and thistles shall it bring forth to thee; and thou shalt eat the herb of the field;

[19] In the sweat of thy face shalt thou eat bread, till thou return unto the ground; for out of it wast thou taken: for dust thou art, and unto dust shalt thou return.

Genesis 3:17-19

---

[20] The Mahabharata of Krishna-Dwaipayana Vyasa, Volume 1 Books 1, 2 and 3 (Kindle Location 23629). . Kindle Edition.

CHAPTER 2

23 Therefore the Lord God sent him forth from the garden of Eden, to till the ground from whence he was taken.

Genesis 3:23

The common interpretation of verse 19, specifically where it says *in the sweat of thy face shalt thou eat bread*, is that Adam would now have to work to prepare his own food. No longer would it be readily available as it was in the Garden of Eden; if Adam wanted bread, he would now have to make it himself. Also, verse 23 states that they had to till the ground. Since tilling ground requires tools and innovation, and since the Serpent was the one who tempted them into this position, it is commonly believed that the development of technology resulted from the influence of the Serpent. If this is to be taken as literal truth, we end up with a very different picture of what is going on with Viswakarma and the Pushpaka.

In *Forbidden Secrets of the Labyrinth*, Mark Flynn talks about how identities can be assigned to mythological characters to see them from a biblical perspective. If ancient mythology is nothing more than a deceptive retelling of the truth from the mouth of the Serpent and his fallen followers, we can see how assigning identities can be useful in reinterpreting these accounts. If we are to believe there is an ancient evil in the world who is trying to subvert the truth in order to fulfill his own goals, we can expect certain reinterpretations of truth to be prevalent.

We can look at this in a couple different ways. Viswakarma could represent YHWH from the view of the Serpent.[21] The Pushpaka could represent the Serpent himself. This could help explain the alternate definition of *serpent* for *puspaka.* Viswakarma constructed the Pushpaka, just as YHWH created the Serpent. However, in the Mahabharata, the Pushpaka was something that was deserving of worship, just as the Serpent seems to believe about himself.

It is also possible that the Serpent is identifying himself with Viswakarma himself. If the Serpent is setting himself up to be the ultimate creator and deity of architects, the Pushpaka could be a representation of the technology he brought into the world. Technology, being a creation of the Serpent (or at the very least a result of the actions of the Serpent), would represent the cunning and wisdom he has. If the Serpent is as self-absorbed as the Bible seems to portray, it would be plausible that he would desire worship, not only for himself, but for his attributes as well.

Setting aside the idea of assigning identities, the story of the Pushpaka brings up some interesting questions. Assuming it was the Serpent who brought technology into the world, would this not mean that technology itself has extradimensional origins? With the influence of the Serpent and other extradimensional beings, how quickly did that technology progress in the ancient

---

[21] YHWH is the name of the God of the Bible.

past? Might ancient man have had access to, or at least encounters with, higher forms of technology than that which is available even today?

Vimanas

Perhaps the most interesting example of possible ancient technology from ancient Sanskrit texts is that of vimanas. Vimanas are mentioned in the Mahabharata. However, in a text called the *Bhagavata Purana*, they are more common.

The Bhagavata Purana primarily focuses on Krishna, the complete incarnation of Lord Vishnu, the Hindu god. We learn of the vimana's capability for flight early on in the Bhagavata Purana:

"As Dhundhukari spoke, a brilliant vimana flew down from the sky, soft as the petals of a rose. In it were many eternal dwellers in Vishnu's realm, Vaikuntha. Dhundhukari embraced his brother Gokarna, and climbed into the ship of the sky."[22]

This vimana, as described, was a true extradimensional vehicle. It is described as flying, but also as carrying the eternal dwellers from Vishnu's realm. We also learn that this vehicle had

---

[22] Menon, Ramesh (2012-11-19). BHAGAVATA PURANA (Kindle Locations 469-471). . Kindle Edition.

physicality to it since Dhundhukari was able to physically climb inside. As described above, this account is not a dream or a vision. This is a description of a personal interaction with an extradimensional vehicle.

To further support the extradimensional properties of these vehicles, another description of the vimana's capabilities is as follows:

"The vimana flashed away into heaven beyond the stars, like a thought, leaving a golden trail in the sky, which dissolved in a few moments and vanished above the perfect silence that had fallen on the gathering of men on the earth below."[23]

We see that the vimana was not only a flying machine of sorts, but was also able to traverse beyond the stars and into heaven. These vehicles were also reported as disk-shaped and having faster-than-light travel: by far a physical impossibility, but something that could be possible if from extradimensional origins:

"I saw Devas fly down to the earth in their mystic vimanas, which are swifter than light."[24]

---

[23] Menon, Ramesh (2012-11-19). BHAGAVATA PURANA (Kindle Locations 478-479). . Kindle Edition.
[24] Menon, Ramesh (2012-11-19). BHAGAVATA PURANA (Kindle Location 561). . Kindle Edition.

"Wondrous Alaka , city of the king of the yakshas and Guhyakas, lord of the Nine Treasures, one of the Lokapalas, the masters of the earth , fairly swarms with vimanas, which look like immense flying jewels, cut like faceted disks, which fly more quickly than light or time. "[25]

The fact the vimanas are described as disk-shaped flying jewels is intriguing when compared to modern-day UFO reports. The reference to them being able to fly faster than light or time is especially interesting. This seems to indicate faster-than-light travel and possibly even time travel. In either case, these capabilities would be more plausible from an extradimensional device rather than extraterrestrial due to the physical laws of nature.[26]

We also learn that these were not only vehicles; they were actually the palaces of extradimensional beings:

"With his yogic powers, Kardama created a fabulous vimana – it was a flying palace! It was surrounded by fine gardens, set with sparkling lakes, and the palace itself was lavished with the nine

---

[25] Menon, Ramesh (2012-11-19). BHAGAVATA PURANA (Kindle Locations 2658-2660). . Kindle Edition.
[26] For more on this, refer to my book *Quantum Creation: Does the Supernatural Lurk in the Fourth Dimension?*, available at www.ministudyministry.com.

precious stones, encrusting the columns that supported the magical edifice."[27]

This flying palace is described as containing *fine gardens, set with sparkling lakes.* This seems to be describing water and plant life. Keeping in mind that vimanas are described as originating from a higher dimension, we can compare this to the Garden of Eden. The Garden of Eden most likely contained extradimensional plant life as well. From this, we can see that the higher dimensions are not only populated with intelligent life, but also with non-intelligent life, such as plants.

We also read of a biblically-familiar ritual that took place before entering the vimana:

"Kardama said to her, 'Go, my love, and bathe in the Bindusaras, before we enter the vimana.'"[28]

This is reminiscent of the rituals the ancient Levitical priests had to perform before being allowed to be in the presence of YHWH, which equates to modern-day baptism in Christianity.[29]

There are many more descriptions of vimanas found all throughout the Bhagavata Purana. To fully appreciate the depth

---

[27] Menon, Ramesh (2012-11-19). BHAGAVATA PURANA (Kindle Locations 1639-1641). . Kindle Edition.
[28] Menon, Ramesh (2012-11-19). BHAGAVATA PURANA (Kindle Locations 1648-1649). . Kindle Edition.
[29] http://www.haydid.org/ronimmer.htm

and vast amount of information, one would have to look at the entire text in full. However, the goal here is not for an exhaustive study of vimanas, extremely interesting though they are. Our goal here is to establish the existence of ancient texts that contain accounts of personal encounters with extradimensional entities and vehicles. As we will see, vimanas are just one description of such vehicles.

Figure 5 - Vishnu and his Avatars, 11th century. Black schist. Brooklyn Museum, Gift of Dr. David R. Nalin, 1991.244.

Vishnu

Vishnu is a Hindu deity of preservation, but what makes this god so interesting are his various avatars (Figure 5). The ten avatars, called the *dashavatara*, are described in an ancient text called the *Puranabharati*. It is said that nine of these avatars have occurred in the past and the final avatar will occur in the future as Kalki. This happens at the end of *Kali Yuga*, which is the last stage of four in a cycle the world goes through. Vishnu descends in the form of the avatar Kalki to restore cosmic order. This is foretold in the Bhagavata Purana:

31

"At that time, the Supreme Personality of Godhead will appear on the earth. Acting with the power of pure spiritual goodness, He will rescue eternal religion. Lord Viṣṇu — the Supreme Personality of Godhead, the spiritual master of all moving and nonmoving living beings, and the Supreme Soul of all — takes birth to protect the principles of religion and to relieve His saintly devotees from the reactions of material work."[30]

The list of avatars varies depending on region and sect, but the standard list is as follows:

1. Matsya: The fish – Vishnu took the form of a fish to warn Vaivasvata of a great flood. Vaivasvata then built a boat to save his family and seven sages. This account is reminiscent of the story of Noah in the book of Genesis.

2. Kurma: The tortoise – The devas and asuras tried to obtain the nectar of immortality by using Mount Mandara to churn the Ocean of Milk. This put the mountain in jeopardy of being destroyed, so Vishnu took the form of a tortoise to support its weight.

3. Vahara: The boar – A demon named Hiranyaksha took the Earth to the bottom of the cosmic ocean. Vishnu took the form of a boar to place the Earth in its original place by carrying it in his tusks after defeating Hiranyaksha.

---

[30] Bhagavata Purana, 12.2.16-17

4. Narasimha: The half man/half lion – The older brother of Hiranyaksha was given a boon from Brahma which made it so he could not be killed by man or animal, inside or out, day or night, on earth or in the stars, with a weapon either living or inanimate. Finding loopholes to all conditions, Vishnu took the form of a human with the head and paws of a lion to kill the evil older brother at the courtyard threshold of his house, at dusk, with his claws, while he lay on his thighs.

5. Vamana: The dwarf – Vishnu descended in the form of a dwarf to petition Bali for three strides of land, only to later turn into a giant, thereby making the strides much larger.

6. Parashurama: The warrior with an axe – Parashurama is the first warrior-saint in Hinduism. He was born of earthly parents and was given an axe by Shiva. He was immortal and is believed to still be alive today in the Mehendra Mountains.

7. Rama: The prince and king of Ayodhya – Sita, the wife of Rama, was taken by the demon king of Lanka, Ravana. Rama defeated the demon king and saved Sita.

8. Krishna: The eighth son of Devaki and Vasudev – Descriptions of Krishna vary; sometimes he is a young child playing a flute or a prince offering guidance. Sometimes he is portrayed as a hero, god-child, or Supreme Being. Krishna is said to ride a chariot pulled by

four horses, which are similar to the horses of Revelation. The rider of the fourth horse of Revelation is Death, yet it also says Hell followed him. It does not describe a fifth horse for Hell to ride, so it is possible these four horses are pulling an unnamed chariot for Hell, thereby giving him a means to follow Death.

9. Buddha: The founder of Buddhism – Descriptions of Buddha vary as well. At times he is seen as leading heretics and demons away from the teaching of the Vedas. Other times he is seen as a teacher of non-violence.

10. Kalki: The final incarnation – Kalki is understood as the final incarnation of Vishnu. It is said he will ride a white horse with a sword that blazes like a comet. Descriptions of Kalki seem to line up with the Islamic end-time figure, especially concerning the white horse, and also the biblical Antichrist as described as the rider of the white horse in chapter six of the book of Revelation.

In 1877, Helena Blavatsky published her first major work, a book entitled *Isis Unveiled*, in which she interpreted the Dashavataras as representing the progression of biological evolution. She interpreted the avatar list as:[31]

1. Matsya - fish, the first class of vertebrates; evolved in water.

---

[31] *Isis Unveiled* by Helena Blavatsky, 1877

2. Kurma - amphibious (living in both water and land; but not to confuse with the vertebrate class amphibians).

3. Varaha - wild land animal.

4. Narasimha - beings that are half-animal and half-human (indicative of emergence of human thoughts and intelligence in powerful wild nature).

5. Vamana - short, premature human beings.

6. Parasurama - early humans living in forests and using weapons.

7. Rama - humans living in community, beginning of civil society.

8. Krishna - humans practicing animal husbandry, politically advanced societies.

9. Buddha - humans finding enlightenment.

10. Kalki - advanced humans with great powers of destruction.

If we look at this from a biblical perspective, we could recognize Vishnu as an extradimensional being; more specifically, a fallen angel. This could explain why Vishnu is sometimes seen as the Supreme Being and why his story inspires ideas such as evolution. This could also explain why he is seen as the individual that will save mankind in the last days, yet descriptions are more similar to the biblical Antichrist. All of these things and more would take away from the true God YHWH by offering an inferior replacement, subverting truth, and leading others astray by keeping them in the bondage of confusion. This would perfectly fit the description of a fallen angel based on biblical descriptions.

After Babel

Why would an angel want to deceive an entire nation? How did they get into a position where they could do such a thing? Is this why there are so many different religions and belief systems?

These questions and more can be answered from understanding an often-overlooked biblical passage. In the King James Version Bible, Deuteronomy 32:8 is translated as:

"When the Most High divided to the nations their inheritance, when he separated the sons of Adam, he set the bounds of the people according to the number of the children of Israel."

The issue here is the last word of the passage. According to the Septuagint and other translations, the phrase *"sons of Israel"* should be translated as *"sons of God"*. The English Standard Version renders it this way:

"When the Most High gave to the nations their inheritance, when he divided mankind, he fixed the borders of the peoples according to the number of the sons of God."

This translation seems to make more sense when we consider the context. This is talking about when God *divided mankind*, which refers back to the tower of Babel. The main reason the *sons of God* translation makes more sense than *sons of Israel* is that at that time (the time right after the tower of Babel), there was no Israel and were no children to be numbered. However, there were definitely sons of God, or what we would call angels.

The short version of the story states that the people of the world, led by the nefarious Nimrod, built the tower in an attempt to enter Heaven and/or petition the fallen angels. They worshipped these fallen angels as their gods, so when YHWH dispersed the people and confused their languages, he did so according to the number of the fallen angels that were worshipped instead of Him. It was basically as if YHWH was saying "Okay, you don't want to worship me, but you want these fallen angels as your gods? Then you can have them over you in your own nations." YHWH has always offered free will to humans and has always provided a way for humans to return to Him if they so choose.

If this is the correct translation, it could help explain the origin of all the world's religions. It could also explain why all other religions offer salvation by personal works, yet biblical text states we cannot attain our own salvation and are in need of a savior. This could also help explain the purpose for the formation of Israel. The verse immediately following what we already looked at, Deuteronomy 32:9, states:

"But the Lord's portion is his people, Jacob his allotted heritage."

YHWH gave the people of the world what they wanted; to worship false and inferior gods. Yet, He still had a plan for people to return if they would so choose. The plan began with YHWH taking His portion, Israel, beginning with Abraham, and later being born in the same lineage as the savior the people of the world required for eternal salvation: Jesus Christ.

Ancient Technology in Antiquity

Denizens of Dimensions Collide

T he account we find in the sixth chapter of Genesis, along with other Jewish sources, is perhaps the most fascinating account of humans interacting with extradimensional beings we have available today. Genesis 6 tell us how the fallen angels descended to procreate with mankind. The offspring created from this forbidden union are known as the Nephilim.[32] The non-canonical book of Enoch gives

---

[32] For more on the Nephilim, refer to my book *Disclosure: Unveiling Our Role in the Secret War of the Ancients.*

us even more details concerning the fallen angels, known as Watchers, and their rebellion against YHWH. Along with their genetic material, we read the Watchers brought other supposed gifts to mankind: technological knowledge.

Inception of Extradimensional Technology

Chapter 7 of the book of Enoch begins to describe what type of knowledge the Watchers brought with them from Heaven:

"And all the others together with them took unto themselves wives, and each chose for himself one, and they began to go in unto them and to defile themselves with them, and they taught them charms and enchantments, and the cutting of roots, and made them acquainted with plants."[33]

The knowledge of roots and plants will be important a bit later. For now, the description of the knowledge handed down from the Watchers is continued in chapter 8:

"And Azazel taught men to make swords, and knives, and shields, and breastplates, and made known to them the metals of the earth and the art of working them, and bracelets, and ornaments, and the use of antimony, and the beautifying of the eyelids, and all kinds of costly stones, and all colouring tinctures. And there arose

---

[33] http://www.hiddenbible.com/enoch/online.html

much godlessness, and they committed fornication, and they were led astray, and became corrupt in all their ways. Semjaza taught enchantments, and root-cuttings, 'Armaros the resolving of enchantments, Baraqijal (taught) astrology, Kokabel the constellations, Ezeqeel the knowledge of the clouds, Araqiel the signs of the earth, Shamsiel the signs of the sun, and Sariel the course of the moon. "[34]

As we compare the biblical book of Genesis with the non-canonical book of Enoch, we find that these events would have occurred just prior to the flood.

Concerning the flood, we find a very interesting account that may help provide a different perspective on how some of these secrets survived. The Jewish historian Josephus writes:

"They [the Children of Seth] also were the inventors of that peculiar sort of wisdom which is concerned with the heavenly bodies, and their order. And that their inventions might not be lost before they were sufficiently known, upon Adam's prediction that the world was to be destroyed at one time by the force of fire, and at another time by the violence and quantity of water, they made two pillars, the one of brick, the other of stone: they inscribed their discoveries on them both, that in case the pillar of brick should be destroyed by the flood, the pillar of stone might remain, and

---

[34] Ibid.

exhibit those discoveries to mankind; and also inform them that there was another pillar of brick erected by them. Now this remains in the land of Siriad [i.e. Egypt] to this day."[35]

The ancient, non-canonical book of Jubilees continues the story:

"And he (Kainam) found a writing which former (generations) had carved on the rock, and he read what was thereon, and he transcribed it and sinned owing to it; for it contained the teaching of the Watchers in accordance with which they used to observe the omens of the sun and moon and stars in all the signs of heaven."[36]

If all of these accounts are to be taken as factual, it may help fill in some blanks and answer some very interesting questions. Was there a type of technology in the antediluvian world? If so, where did it come from? Did it survive the worldwide flood?

The Sphinx and Great Pyramid Speculation

According to the account of Josephus and the book of Jubilees, there is not much information given about the pillars of the children of Seth. We are told that there were two pillars, one of brick and one of stone. They were not sure if the pillar of brick

---

[35] Flavius Josephus, *Antiquities of the Jews,* (1-2-3) translation by William Whiston
[36] The Book of Jubilees, chapter 8, verse 3

would be destroyed by the flood, so in case it was, they built the pillar of stone and inscribed their discoveries on both. We are told that at least the pillar of stone remained in Egypt, at least in the days of Josephus (37-100 A.D.). We are also told that these pillars contained the teaching of the Watchers and it was considered sinful to follow these teachings. This begs the question, is there anything in Egypt today that may point to more answers concerning these pillars?

What is presented here is certainly speculative, but it is interesting nevertheless and may provide clues to our ancient past. There is a possibility the two pillars could actually be the Great Pyramid and what is now the Great Sphinx in Egypt. Author and researcher Robert M. Schoch has postulated, due to the evidence of water erosion, the Great Sphinx of Giza is far older than most suspect and that a catastrophe of some kind destroyed any other evidence of an older civilization. Schoch's research was showcased in the 1993 documentary *Mystery of the Sphinx*, presented by Charlton Heston. In *Mystery of the Sphinx*, the idea is put forth that the Sphinx was originally nothing more than a large, natural stone jutting from the earth. An unknown civilization saw the stone and decided to carve into it, yet what they carved originally is also unknown. After the unknown civilization was destroyed, a new civilization arrived and carved the stone into the figure of a head. Also, a body was dug out and formed from the ground underneath. Thus, the Sphinx we see today was created.

If there is any validity to this idea, it may help explain the pillar of stone that contained the teaching of the Watchers. It is possible the stone that was found originally was inscribed with these teachings, then the flood came. Later civilizations then, for reasons unknown (possibly due to the actions of Kainam), removed the inscriptions by carving the stone down to the image of a head. They may have created the body to form a complete cherub-like statue in order to protect something. This could be the pillar of stone.

The pillar of brick, then, could be the Great Pyramid; specifically the missing capstone. There is certainly a lot of information and speculation that can be looked at in regards to the Great Pyramid. For our purposes here, we can just look at the theory that the Great Pyramid could be made of brick and, if the builders were unsure if it would survive the flood, it might make sense they would inscribe the teaching of the Watchers at the very top: the capstone.[37] What exactly happened to the capstone, why it is missing today, and if it is still in existence somewhere is up for debate.

---

[37] Stating the Great Pyramid is made from formed brick and not quarried stone is controversial. For an interesting post concerning this, visit http://io9.com/5869417/what-are-the-great-pyramids-really-made-out-of

Of course, when talking about these possibilities, there are many theories; each one more speculative than the last. However, I do believe truth can be found somewhere between all of these theories. At the very least, it is certainly an intriguing subject. There is a wide variety of resources available to those who are interested in this topic. For more information about the biblical connection to the mysteries of the Great Pyramid, I highly recommend the book *The Great Pyramid: Prophecy in Stone* by Noah Hutchings.

Nephilim Grapes

The accounts we looked at earlier may help to explain a very strange verse in the biblical book of Numbers:

"And they came unto the brook of Eshcol, and cut down from thence a branch with one cluster of grapes, and they bare it between two upon a staff; and they brought of the pomegranates, and of the figs."

Numbers 13:23

These grapes were found in the land of the post-flood giants. The most obvious questions that comes to mind concerns the size of these grapes. If it took two normal-sized men to carry one cluster, how big were these grapes and how did they grow so large?

Explanations of this verse range widely from person to person. Some form speculations about ancient genetic engineering while others will diminish the grapes themselves to normal-sized. Personally, I'm not sure if there is sufficient evidence to say the grapes were genetically engineered (though I'm also not completely counting that out), but I also do not believe these were normal-sized grapes due to the description of how they were carried. Even the Israeli Ministry of Tourism logo shows larger-than-normal grapes in its depiction of this event (Figure 6). Also, Numbers 13:24 tells us that the place was named Eschol (meaning "cluster") because

Figure 6 - Israeli Ministry of Tourism Logo

of the cluster of grapes.[38] If these were normal grapes, it certainly would not seem to be worth naming the land after, especially considering they took more fruit than only grapes. There was something that set these specific grapes apart, and it seems to be their enormous size.

---

[38] "Hebrew Lexicon :: H812 (KJV)." Blue Letter Bible. Accessed 6 Dec, 2014. http://www.blueletterbible.org/lang/Lexicon/Lexicon.cfm?Strongs=H812&t= KJV

The Canopy Theory

There might be another explanation as to how the grapes grew to such large size. The canopy theory states that before the worldwide flood, there was a vast amount of water (usually either in the form of vapor or ice) that covered the atmosphere of the entire earth. It is speculated that this canopy resulted in a higher concentration of oxygen and air pressure throughout the world. It is also said these conditions would allow for things to grow much larger in size. The theory explains that this canopy would have come down during the flood and would have contributed to the water that drowned the world.

There might be scientific evidence showing things actually do grow larger in canopy-like conditions. In 2006, insect physiologist Alexander Kaiser and his colleagues compared four species of beetle and, based on their calculations, were able to show that modern beetles could grow to as much as six inches with increased oxygen.[39] This could help explain why things seem so much larger in the antediluvian world.

Of course, if the canopy theory is correct, the atmospheric water that would have created those conditions would have fallen during the flood. The passage we look at in the book of Numbers took place well after the flood. The canopy theory in and of itself cannot explain the size of the grapes, but it might provide a clue.

---

[39] http://www.livescience.com/1083-oxygen-giant-bugs.html

It is possible the ancient giants of Eschol found a way to recreate the conditions of the antediluvian world to make their crops grow larger. This would require a certain level of technology, of course, but not as much as would genetic engineering. We are even doing things like this today with hyperbaric therapy.[40] This, among other things we looked at in this chapter, could help provide evidence supporting the existence of technology in our ancient past.

Interview with Cris Putnam

 While considering possible scenarios, especially with something as speculative and controversial as ancient technology, it is of great benefit to gain perspectives from other noted researchers. Cris Putnam is a bestselling author and Christian apologist. He holds a Masters in Theological Studies, a Certification in Christian Apologetics, and a B.S. in religion and mathematics. He has been interviewed on Prophecy in the News numerous times as well as the television show *Countdown to Apocalypse* on The History Channel. He has appeared on major radio shows and podcasts across the country. Cris is the author of The Supernatural Worldview as well as the coauthor of Petrus Romanus and Exo-Vaticana alongside Thomas

---

[40] http://hyperbaricmedicalsolutions.com/

Horn. I first met Cris in person at The Prophecy Forum conference in Dublin, Ohio in November of 2014. After speaking with him about the possibilities of ancient technology, it became apparent he would be a great resource for this type of study. As special thanks goes out to Cris for taking the time to participate in this interview.

*   *   *

JOSH PECK: Do you believe ancient technologies may have existed in the antediluvian and/or post-flood world, and if so, in what form?

CRIS PUTNAM: It depends on what one means by "technology." In a general sense, any tool (like a hammer or the wheel) is a form of technology. So the answer is obviously yes. If you mean computers, electrical devices, and nuclear weapons as implied by ancient astronaut theory then I think not. That said, scholars are still troubled by megaliths like the Great Pyramid even though reasonable theories have been offered that do not involve high technology. For example, ancient art depicts the use of wooden sleds (low technology) to move blocks the size and shape of the ones used for the pyramid.[41] Even so, I am certainly open to the idea that ancient people accessed the supernatural realm facilitating various paranormal phenomenon but this is extremely hard to prove. The pyramid itself seems to be a piece of "spiritual technology" for allowing the deceased Pharaoh to access the underworld successfully.

JOSH PECK: What do you believe was the source of ancient technological knowledge?

CRIS PUTNAM: In the case of the wooden sleds above, it was largely human ingenuity but this does not rule out things like divine revelation. For example, Noah was given specific instructions to build a huge ark. Of course this large boat is a piece of technology. Given the immense size of the Great Pyramid, it seems fair to speculate the ancient Egyptians (or their predecessors) also received instructions from an otherworldly source.

JOSH PECK: What biblical evidence is there to support your opinion?

CRIS PUTNAM: Specific instructions for Noah's ark are given by Yahweh to Noah in Genesis 6:14-17. Also Solomon was given

---

[41] Dieter Arnold. "Building in Egypt; Pharaonic Stone Masonry." Building in Egypt; Pharaonic Stone Masonry, n.d. http://hbar.phys.msu.ru/gorm/ahist/arnold/arnold.htm

specific instructions concerning the temple which is arguably an example of sacred technology (1 Kings 6:19; 8:6; 2 Chronicles 2:1 ff).

JOSH PECK: Outside of the Bible, what historical or archaeological evidence is there to support your opinion?

CRIS PUTNAM: The ark's design has been tested by modern ship builders and it is incredibly seaworthy. Johan Huibers built a replica according to the original biblical description that is docked in the Netherlands.[42] The existence of similar pyramids worldwide suggests that ancient people were instructed by spirit beings (angels) and the correlated practice of human sacrifice suggests these were fallen angels who accepted worship as gods.

JOSH PECK: Do you believe ancient technologies have influenced the course of our modern world in any way, and if so, how?

CRIS PUTNAM: This seems rather obvious because all scientific and technological innovation begins with what came before. In our ancient past, man began to use the wheel and this progressed from crude wheelbarrows and carts to the modern automobile. This suggests a similar progression has ensued in occult "science" as

---

[42] David Moye, "Noah's Ark Replica Made By Johan Huibers Opens Doors In Dordrecht, Netherlands" Huffington Post http://www.huffingtonpost.com/2012/07/30/noahs-ark-replica-johan-huibers-netherlands_n_1717778.html

well but, of course, by its very nature this information is kept secret. It is interesting to note that modern materialist science grew out of hermeticism and alchemy. After purchasing and studying Isaac Newton's alchemical works in 1942, economist John Maynard Keynes argued that "Newton was not the first of the age of reason, he was the last of the magicians."[43]

*　　*　　*

Cris Putnam has a wealth of information that everyone interested should look into. Make sure to check out *The Supernatural Worldview* by Cris Putnam.[44] Visit www.SupernaturalWorldview.com and www.LogosApologia.org to find out more about Cris and his ministry.

---

[43] John Maynard Keynes: Newton, the Man http://www-history.mcs.st-and.ac.uk/Extras/Keynes_Newton.html
[44] Available at http://www.amazon.com/Supernatural-Worldview-Examining-Paranormal-Apocalyptic/dp/0985604565

Hebrew Visions of Chariots

Who Saw the Chariots?

Visions of heavenly chariots can be found in a few places throughout ancient Hebrew texts. Probably the most famous visions of heavenly chariots are those of the prophets Ezekiel and Zechariah. We will get to those a bit later. For now, as a precursor, we can look at some of the other visions of chariots found in Jewish Scripture.

Elijah and Elisha

One of the most dramatic visions of extradimensional chariots can be found in the pages of the Bible concerning the prophet Elijah. We read in 2 Kings:

"And it came to pass, when the Lord would take up Elijah into heaven by a whirlwind, that Elijah went with Elisha from Gilgal."

2 Kings 2:1

We find out later, as this verse implies, it was known to the sons of the prophets that Elijah would be taken into heaven by a whirlwind.[45] Elijah clearly knew this as well. This foreknowledge isn't recorded as a prophecy in the Bible, but it seems there existed an unrecorded prophecy that was common knowledge to the sons of the prophets.

The Bible gives some very interesting detail as to how this extradimensional encounter happened. Later in 2 Kings, we read:

And it came to pass, as they still went on, and talked, that, behold, there appeared a chariot of fire, and horses of fire, and parted them both asunder; and Elijah went up by a whirlwind into heaven.

2 Kings 2:11

---

[45] 2 Kings 2:3, 2 Kings 2:5

We learn that not only was there a chariot of fire, but horses of fire as well. These all took part in taking Elijah into, what is described as, a whirlwind. This whirlwind, as we will see in later chapters, is common in biblical descriptions of heavenly chariots. It is possible this whirlwind is not just a mere tornado or other type of natural storm; this type of heavenly whirlwind seems to be a type of interdimensional portal between our world and the higher dimensions.

Another point of interest, as we will look at deeper in the next chapter, is what Elisha exclaims as he sees Elijah taken up into the whirlwind:

And Elisha saw it, and he cried, My father, my father, the chariot of Israel, and the horsemen thereof. And he saw him no more: and he took hold of his own clothes, and rent them in two pieces.

2 Kings 2:12

In verse 11, it says there were horses present. In verse 12, Elisha makes mention of *horsemen*, signifying there were other beings present apart from the horses. This is a theme we see repeated in the account of Zechariah, which we will look at a bit later.

What's also interesting is that Elisha refers to this vehicle as the chariot of Israel. This seems to be the official extradimensional vehicle of Israel that God uses as is needed. We will see further physical descriptions of this vehicle when we look into the account of the prophet Ezekiel.

Later on in his life, Elisha sees manifestations of higher dimensions again. When the servant saw that he and Elisha were surrounded by the natural, worldly horses and chariots of the enemy, Elisha did not seem worried at all. When the servant's fears were made known to him, Elisha did the sensible thing:

And Elisha prayed, and said, Lord, I pray thee, open his eyes, that he may see. And the Lord opened the eyes of the young man; and he saw: and, behold, the mountain was full of horses and chariots of fire round about Elisha.

2 Kings 6:17

We see here again a reference to horses and chariots of fire. This is another example of beings from a higher dimension interacting with the affairs of human beings from our world in the ancient past.

Enoch

Though not a part of canon, the book of Enoch details a very interesting encounter with a human and extradimensional entities. The Bible itself provides a limited amount of information concerning Enoch:

CHAPTER 4

²¹ And Enoch lived sixty and five years, and begat Methuselah:

²² And Enoch walked with God after he begat Methuselah three hundred years, and begat sons and daughters:

²³ And all the days of Enoch were three hundred sixty and five years:

²⁴ And Enoch walked with God: and he was not; for God took him.

Genesis 5:21-24

Verse 24 is the end of the Genesis description of what happened to Enoch. Luckily the author of the book of Hebrews gives us a bit more information:

"By faith Enoch was translated that he should not see death; and was not found, because God had translated him: for before his translation he had this testimony, that he pleased God."

Hebrews 11:5

We read that Enoch was *translated* and did not experience death. The word "translated" is interesting: it comes from the Greek word *"metatithēmi"* and means *"to transpose (two things, one of which is put in place of the other), to transfer, to change"*.[46] It is

---

[46] "Greek Lexicon :: G3346 (KJV)." Blue Letter Bible. Accessed 21 Dec, 2014. http://www.blueletterbible.org/lang/Lexicon/Lexicon.cfm?Strongs=G3346&t=KJV

theorized that this is a precursor to the same type of change or transfer that will happen to all believers when Jesus Christ returns.

The book of Enoch gives us a wealth of information about Enoch's encounter with extradimensional entities. The best chance we have at trying to envision what Enoch saw is to read the account itself:

"Behold, in the vision clouds invited me and a mist summoned me, and the course of the stars and the lightnings sped and hastened me, and the winds in the vision caused me to fly and lifted me upward, and bore me into heaven. And I went in till I drew nigh to a wall which is built of crystals and surrounded by tongues of fire: and it began to affright me. And I went into the tongues of fire and drew nigh to a large house which was built of crystals: and the walls of the house were like a tesselated floor (made) of crystals, and its groundwork was of crystal. Its ceiling was like the path of the stars and the lightnings, and between them were fiery cherubim, and their heaven was (clear as) water. A flaming fire surrounded the walls, and its portals blazed with fire. And I entered into that house, and it was hot as fire and cold as ice: there were no delights of life therein: fear covered me, and trembling got hold upon me. And as I quaked and trembled, I fell upon my face. And I beheld a vision, And lo! there was a second house, greater than the former, and the entire portal stood open before me, and it was built of flames of fire. And in every respect

it so excelled in splendour and magnificence and extent that I cannot describe to you its splendour and its extent. And its floor was of fire, and above it were lightnings and the path of the stars, and its ceiling also was flaming fire. And I looked and saw therein a lofty throne: its appearance was as crystal, and the wheels thereof as the shining sun, and there was the vision of cherubim. And from underneath the throne came streams of flaming fire so that I could not look thereon. And the Great Glory sat thereon, and His raiment shone more brightly than the sun and was whiter than any snow. None of the angels could enter and could behold His face by reason of the magnificence and glory and no flesh could behold Him. The flaming fire was round about Him, and a great fire stood before Him, and none around could draw nigh Him: ten thousand times ten thousand (stood) before Him, yet He needed no counselor. And the most holy ones who were nigh to Him did not leave by night nor depart from Him. And until then I had been prostrate on my face, trembling: and the Lord called me with His own mouth, and said to me: ' Come hither, Enoch, and hear my word.' And one of the holy ones came to me and waked me, and He made me rise up and approach the door: and I bowed my face downwards. "[47]

At first, in the beginning of this account, we get the sense this is nothing more than a vision of some sort. However, at the end of

---

[47] The Book of Enoch 14:8-25 - http://www.hiddenbible.com/enoch/online.html

this passage, we read that, by the command of the Lord, one of the holy ones woke Enoch to approach the door so Enoch could see the vision was depicting reality. It is possible that this was more than just a dream from God. It is possible that, since Enoch was experiencing something outside from our three spatial dimensions, he was taken out of his three-dimensional body. Instead of the vehicle coming to meet Enoch, it seems as though God brought Enoch up to the higher dimensions.

Elijah and Enoch: The Two Witnesses?

There is a common belief in Christianity that the prophetic two witnesses of Revelation are, in fact, Elijah and Enoch. On the surface, this seems plausible since Elijah and Enoch have never died. Some will also speculate the identity of the two witnesses is Elijah and Moses. On the surface, this also seems plausible since Elijah and Moses were seen on the Mount of Transfiguration.[48] Are the two witnesses, in fact, interdimensional, or even extradimensional, beings?

To answer this, we need only to take a deeper look at the text in question:

---

[48] Matthew 17:3

CHAPTER 4

³ And I will give power unto my two witnesses, and they shall prophesy a thousand two hundred and threescore days, clothed in sackcloth.

⁴ These are the two olive trees, and the two candlesticks standing before the God of the earth.

⁵ And if any man will hurt them, fire proceedeth out of their mouth, and devoureth their enemies: and if any man will hurt them, he must in this manner be killed.

⁶ These have power to shut heaven, that it rain not in the days of their prophecy: and have power over waters to turn them to blood, and to smite the earth with all plagues, as often as they will.

⁷ And when they shall have finished their testimony, the beast that ascendeth out of the bottomless pit shall make war against them, and shall overcome them, and kill them.

⁸ And their dead bodies shall lie in the street of the great city, which spiritually is called Sodom and Egypt, where also our Lord was crucified.

⁹ And they of the people and kindreds and tongues and nations shall see their dead bodies three days and an half, and shall not suffer their dead bodies to be put in graves.

[10] And they that dwell upon the earth shall rejoice over them, and make merry, and shall send gifts one to another; because these two prophets tormented them that dwelt on the earth.

[11] And after three days and an half the spirit of life from God entered into them, and they stood upon their feet; and great fear fell upon them which saw them.

[12] And they heard a great voice from heaven saying unto them, Come up hither. And they ascended up to heaven in a cloud; and their enemies beheld them.

Revelation 11:3-12

There is a lot of information here; more than enough to warrant a deep, in-depth, and exhaustive study. However, for our purposes here, we need only to consider a few main points.

We read that these two men will have special abilities, such as breathing fire, causing droughts, and turning water to blood. This easily could cause the reader to assume these two men are Elijah and Moses, as they are credited for similar acts during their lives. However, we must remember that ultimately, this type of power comes from God Himself and is not necessarily a natural ability these men have.

We also read, what I consider to be, the key detail given to tell us if these men are in fact Moses, Elijah, or Enoch. We read that the beast will overcome and kill the two witnesses. After three and a half days, they will rise from the dead and ascend into Heaven. Death and resurrection are the two main details to find out who these men are.

Automatically, in my humble opinion, we can rule Moses out. Moses already lived and died. The book of Hebrews tells us:

"And as it is appointed unto men once to die, but after this the judgment:"

Hebrews 9:27

Moses already died once. Therefore, if Hebrews 9:27 is to be correct, he could not die again.

What then of Enoch and Elijah? We already looked at passages that tell us neither of them died physically but were instead taken up into Heaven. Are they waiting in Heaven for their chance to die? The book of 1 Corinthians tells us:

"Now this I say, brethren, that flesh and blood cannot inherit the kingdom of God; neither doth corruption inherit incorruption."

1 Corinthians 15:50

Flesh and blood, biological physicality as we know it, cannot inherit the kingdom of God. This is why Enoch (and presumably Elijah) were translated. They were given new, extradimensional bodies so they could enter Heaven and be face to face with God, supported by what God Himself said:

"And he said, Thou canst not see my face: for there shall no man see me, and live."

Exodus 33:20

Therefore, Elijah and Enoch never knew death and will never know death. They have already been translated. The two witnesses have not been translated yet as this is written to happen after they die and are resurrected. Elijah and Enoch, already in their new bodies, cannot be killed.

You might be wondering, well who then are the two witnesses? I often wonder that myself, if I am being perfectly honest. While we may not know their true identity, there are things we can know about them. They are not eternal. They have the ability to die. They will be resurrected after they die. While it is not outside of the realm of possibility that there are other aspects to this that may still allow for Enoch, Elijah, or Moses to be the two witnesses, I believe it is far more likely based on Scripture that the two witnesses will be normal human beings who are given great power from the Almighty. In my opinion, they will most likely be born into our time or the near future and live a normal, three-dimensional existence until it is time for them to fulfill God's purposes. When we look at biblical accounts of extradimensional beings, I do not believe the two witnesses can fit the bill. Though they will be extraordinary indeed, I believe they

CHAPTER 4

will be regular human beings given power from the ultimate extradimensional source: the one, true, living God.

CHERUBIM CHARIOTS

Visions through Time and Space

The Prophet Zechariah

One of the most astounding accounts of extradimensional vehicles was described by the Hebrew prophet Zechariah. What makes Zechariah's account so phenomenal is not only the descriptions of heavenly chariots, but also the prophetic nature of his writing. Zechariah saw things that would happen in the future; even on into our own future. The books of Zechariah and Ezekiel could be considered as going hand in hand when we consider the amount of prophecy and the similarities in the accounts of extradimensional encounters. We will look into the book of Ezekiel in the next chapter, but first we will consider the information Zechariah provides.

The Scroll

We find an interesting account of Zechariah's vision of a flying scroll in Scripture:

5:1 Then I turned, and lifted up mine eyes, and looked, and behold a flying roll.

2 And he said unto me, What seest thou? And I answered, I see a flying roll; the length thereof is twenty cubits, and the breadth thereof ten cubits.

3 Then said he unto me, This is the curse that goeth forth over the face of the whole earth: for every one that stealeth shall be cut off as on this side according to it; and every one that sweareth shall be cut off as on that side according to it.

4 I will bring it forth, saith the Lord of hosts, and it shall enter into the house of the thief, and into the house of him that sweareth falsely by my name: and it shall remain in the midst of his house, and shall consume it with the timber thereof and the stones thereof.

Zechariah 5:1-4

CHAPTER 5

Zechariah 5:1 tells us that Zechariah looked up and saw something called a *"flying roll"*. The word *"roll"* comes from the Hebrew word *"megillah"* meaning *"roll, book, writing"*.[49] This is not referring to a literal book as we would think of a book today. This is referring to a scroll. In technical terms, what we would consider as a *"book"* is actually a *"codex"*.[50] A *"book"* in ancient times would be in reference to a scroll. Also interesting to note is the Hebrew word used for *"flying"* could also imply a type of hovering.[51] Quite simply, Zechariah saw a scroll flying or hovering in the air.

In Zechariah 5:2, we learn the measurements of this flying scroll. We are told that the scroll is twenty cubits in length and ten cubits in breadth. It is very interesting that the exact measurement of the flying scroll is given. What is equally as interesting is that Zechariah knew what the exact measurement was just by looking at it. When we look deeper, we realize why:

6:14 And the elders of the Jews builded, and they prospered through the prophesying of Haggai the prophet and Zechariah the son of

---

[49] "Hebrew Lexicon :: H4039 (KJV)." Blue Letter Bible. Accessed 23 Nov, 2013.
http://www.blueletterbible.org/lang/Lexicon/Lexicon.cfm?Strongs=H4039&t=KJV

[50] codex.- Dictionary.com. *Dictionary.com Unabridged*. Random House, Inc. http://dictionary.reference.com/browse/codex (accessed: November 23, 2013).

[51] "Hebrew Lexicon :: H5774 (KJV)." Blue Letter Bible. Accessed 23 Nov, 2013.
http://www.blueletterbible.org/lang/Lexicon/Lexicon.cfm?Strongs=H5774&t=KJV

Iddo. And they builded, and finished it, according to the commandment of the God of Israel, and according to the commandment of Cyrus, and Darius, and Artaxerxes king of Persia.

Ezra 6:14

This is speaking of the building of the second Jewish Temple. What we find out is Zechariah was present at the building and, along with Haggai, he prophesied over the elders of the Jews while they built. Given his job, the amount of involvement he had, and all of the scriptural references, it is reasonable to assume Zechariah would have been well aware of the measurements used in the building of the temple.

1 Kings 6:3 tells us that the porch of Solomon's temple was twenty cubits by ten cubits. Given Zechariah was associated with the building of the second temple and he would have been aware of this measurement, we begin to realize how Zechariah was able to immediately know the exact measurements of the flying scroll. He recognized the size of the scroll as matching the size of the porch of the temple. 1 Kings 7:7 also tells us that it was from the porch, called the porch of judgment, where Solomon would judge. This has great significance when considering the meaning of Zechariah's vision of the flying scroll.

In Zechariah 5:3, Zechariah is told that the scroll is *"the curse that goeth forth over the face of the whole earth"*. It is important to note that this curse was not only for Israel. This curse was meant for the entire population of planet Earth. We are told that *"for every one that stealeth shall be cut off as on this side according to it; and every one that sweareth shall be cut off as on that side according to it."* This is a judgment for two very specific sins: stealing and swearing. The judgment of being *"cut off"* is not the same as we would normally think. Usually, when we think of cut off, we think of a type of execution. Here, however, the Hebrew word used for *"cut off"* is *"naqah"* meaning *"to be cleaned out, be purged out"*.[52] The implication here is that whoever will commit these sins will be utterly wiped out; collectively and completely cleared out of the way. It is a far harsher judgment than just a single, personal execution of sorts. It is more of a purification process for the entire Earth to remove those who commit these sins.

The two sins mentioned here are especially interesting. Considering the first sin mentioned, the word *"stealeth"* comes from the Hebrew word *"ganab"* meaning *"to steal, steal away, carry away"*.[53] The word *"sweareth"* comes from the Hebrew

---

[52] "Hebrew Lexicon :: H5352 (KJV)." Blue Letter Bible. Accessed 23 Nov, 2013.
http://www.blueletterbible.org/lang/Lexicon/Lexicon.cfm?Strongs=H5352&t=KJV
[53] "Hebrew Lexicon :: H1589 (KJV)." Blue Letter Bible. Accessed 23 Nov, 2013.
http://www.blueletterbible.org/lang/Lexicon/Lexicon.cfm?Strongs=H1589&t=KJV

word *"shaba"* meaning *"to swear, to curse"*.[54] These Hebrew words are signifying the sins of stealing and cursing. We learn that each sin is judged from either side of the flying scroll.

What is important to note is that in ancient Israel, scrolls would be written on only one side. This scroll, however, is written on two sides. There are various shadows that can be looked at through this understanding. The first, and probably most important, shadow that can be found is that of the Ten Commandments. The twentieth chapter of the book of Exodus gives us the Ten Commandments in their proper order. We must remember that the Ten Commandments were presented on two slabs of stone. There were five commandments on each slab. This could be a direct shadow to the two sides of the flying scroll. To further support this, if we look at the very center of each slab, the middle commandment in each list of five, we see an interesting parallel. The third commandment, being the very middle of the first slab of stone, is the commandment against taking the name of the Lord in vain. Essentially, this is referring to cursing against God or falsely swearing His name. The eighth commandment, being the middle of the second slab of stone, is the commandment against stealing. The sins of cursing and stealing are the very sins

---

[54] "Hebrew Lexicon :: H7650 (KJV)." Blue Letter Bible. Accessed 23 Nov, 2013.
http://www.blueletterbible.org/lang/Lexicon/Lexicon.cfm?Strongs=H7650&t=KJV

that the flying scroll is sent to bring judgment upon. The flying scroll could be considered a shadow of the Ten Commandments.

Clearly, the God of the Bible is not limited. Many times, He will have a single object be a shadow of many different things, but still with a common thread or theme connecting them. That seems to be what we have here with the flying scroll. When we go back to the idea of the scroll being written on both sides, we can find even more shadows throughout the Bible. We can look to Ezekiel for an example of this:

7 And thou shalt speak my words unto them, whether they will hear, or whether they will forbear: for they are most rebellious.

8 But thou, son of man, hear what I say unto thee; Be not thou rebellious like that rebellious house: open thy mouth, and eat that I give thee.

9 And when I looked, behold, an hand was sent unto me; and, lo, a roll of a book was therein;

10 And he spread it before me; and it was written within and without: and there was written therein lamentations, and mourning, and woe.

3 Moreover he said unto me, Son of man, eat that thou findest; eat this roll, and go speak unto the house of Israel.

2 So I opened my mouth, and he caused me to eat that roll.

³ And he said unto me, Son of man, cause thy belly to eat, and fill thy bowels with this roll that I give thee. Then did I eat it; and it was in my mouth as honey for sweetness.

⁴ And he said unto me, Son of man, go, get thee unto the house of Israel, and speak with my words unto them.

Ezekiel 2:7-3:4

Ezekiel was given a scroll that was written on both sides, just like the flying scroll Zechariah saw. Ezekiel was commanded to eat this scroll, which was as sweet as honey. It was through the eating of this scroll that Ezekiel was able to speak with the words of God Himself. Ezekiel's scroll, in essence, was the Word of God. We can clearly see that Zechariah's flying scroll contained the Word of God as well.

This is also reminiscent of another scroll mentioned in the book of Revelation:

⁸ And the voice which I heard from heaven spake unto me again, and said, Go and take the little book which is open in the hand of the angel which standeth upon the sea and upon the earth.

⁹ And I went unto the angel, and said unto him, Give me the little book. And he said unto me, Take it, and eat it up; and it shall make thy belly bitter, but it shall be in thy mouth sweet as honey.

¹⁰ And I took the little book out of the angel's hand, and ate it up; and it was in my mouth sweet as honey: and as soon as I had eaten it, my belly was bitter.

¹¹ And he said unto me, Thou must prophesy again before many peoples, and nations, and tongues, and kings.

Revelation 10:8-11

This is another important shadow to consider. John was commanded to eat the book, which is the same thing as a scroll in this passage, and it was as sweet as honey. We also learn that it was bitter in John's stomach. This scroll, just like the scroll Ezekiel was commanded to eat, allowed John to prophesy to the whole world. The only difference is that Ezekiel's scroll was only to prophesy to Israel, whereas John's was to prophesy to the entire world. That might be the reason that John's scroll became bitter in his stomach. It could be that the importance and burden was heavier because it was for the entire world at the last of the last times. In that sense, we can see the scroll of Ezekiel meant to prophesy to Israel as a shadow for the future scroll of John that would be meant to prophesy to the entire world.

The last shadow we will look at for the flying scroll of Zechariah is found in the fifth chapter of Revelation:

"And I saw in the right hand of him that sat on the throne a book written within and on the backside, sealed with seven seals."

Revelation 5:1

Again, just like Revelation 10, the book here is actually a scroll. The first thing to notice is this scroll is written on both sides, just as are the flying scroll of Zechariah and the scroll of Ezekiel. When reading the entire chapter, we discover that it is Jesus who possesses this scroll. The scroll is sealed by seven seals which represent judgments to come upon the earth as each seal is broken. The idea of judgment can tie back to Solomon's porch of judgment and the measurement of Zechariah's scroll. Zechariah's vision could be a shadow of the scroll in Revelation 5 since it is described as being written on both sides and bringing about judgment.

As a quick side note, we read in Revelation 5:6 that the Lamb Jesus had seven eyes, which represent His seven spirits. This could have something to do with the stone in Zechariah 3:9, which is also described as having seven eyes. This is a possibility because the stone in Zechariah is said to be engraved, much like in Revelation 2:17 where we are told of the white stone that contains a new name for those who receive it. Zechariah 3:8 makes mention of Jesus Christ as the Branch. The very next verse describes the stone with seven eyes, as well as mentions that God will remove the iniquity of the land in that day. Comparing that with Revelation, we can see the similarities.

Going back to the flying scroll of Zechariah, we can realize that this scroll is not mentioned as having any kind of seals attached, such as the one in the book of Revelation. Since the scroll in Zechariah is already bringing about judgment, it would be reasonable to assume that the seals have already been broken; the flying scroll is not bound by the seals. This makes sense due to the fact that the scroll is sent to execute a judgment of a complete purging of the sinners on Earth. This could be a direct reference to the Day of the Lord.

Zechariah saw the scroll flying/hovering for some time before judgment came. This means there could have been time for other events to transpire within the prophetic timeline as described in Revelation. This would seem to make sense given Zechariah's next vision. The second vision that completes the fifth chapter of Zechariah is the vision of the ephah.

The Ephah

The vision of the ephah and the vision of the flying scroll have both had their fair share of speculation throughout history. Nowadays, certain people attribute the vision of the scroll and the vision of the ephah to UFOs and other related things. While I personally may not see evidence to support the idea of the flying scroll representing a type of UFO or chariot, I do see possible scriptural evidence for that conclusion in the vision of the ephah.

That possible evidence to show the ephah may have been an extradimensional vehicle for an extradimensional being is what we will explore in this section. We will even see the influence of additional extradimensional beings acting as external pilots to this ephah-craft in this passage. Continuing from where we left off in the book of Zechariah:

5 Then the angel that talked with me went forth, and said unto me, Lift up now thine eyes, and see what is this that goeth forth.

6 And I said, What is it? And he said, This is an ephah that goeth forth. He said moreover, This is their resemblance through all the earth.

7 And, behold, there was lifted up a talent of lead: and this is a woman that sitteth in the midst of the ephah.

8 And he said, This is wickedness. And he cast it into the midst of the ephah; and he cast the weight of lead upon the mouth thereof.

9 Then lifted I up mine eyes, and looked, and, behold, there came out two women, and the wind was in their wings; for they had wings like the wings of a stork: and they lifted up the ephah between the earth and the heaven.

10 Then said I to the angel that talked with me, Whither do these bear the ephah?

CHAPTER 5

[11] And he said unto me, To build it an house in the land of Shinar: and it shall be established, and set there upon her own base.

Zechariah 5:5-11

Verses five and six give us the basic setup of the vision. Zechariah sees an ephah moving through the sky and he is told *"this is their resemblance through all the earth"*. A very interesting thing to note is the word used for *"resemblance"* can also just as easily mean *"eye"*, and even some noted theologians have thought this to be the case.[55] If this is referring to *"eye"* instead of *"resemblance"*, it adds a whole new dimension to the passage. Some have attributed this to depictions of the all-seeing eye connected to the Illuminati. Others would take this back to the idea of Satan and his "eye", whose establishment is destroyed by the Hand of God. This is the message that is found when we consider the meanings of each Hebrew letter that make up the name of Yeshua (Jesus).

Each Hebrew letter has its own unique meaning. When you have a Hebrew word, there is contained the meaning of the word, but also the meaning of each letter that makes up the word to add further insight. The Hebrew name of Jesus is Yeshua, which is made up of the Hebrew letters Yod, Shin, Vav, and Ayin. Yod

---

[55] "Hebrew Lexicon :: H5869 (KJV)." Blue Letter Bible. Accessed 24 Nov, 2013.
http://www.blueletterbible.org/lang/Lexicon/Lexicon.cfm?Strongs=H5869&t=KJV

means *"hand"*, Shin means *"destroy"*, Vav means *"establishment"*, and Ayin means *"eye"*.[56] This can be shown further in scripture:

"He that committeth sin is of the devil; for the devil sinneth from the beginning. For this purpose the Son of God was manifested, that he might destroy the works of the devil."

1 John 3:8

Also interesting to note, the word used for *"resemblance"* is the same Hebrew word/letter *"ayin"*: the last letter in the Hebrew name of Jesus meaning *"eye"*. If this ephah is *"their eye"* instead of *"their resemblance"*, then we have something very interesting. While *"their"* is plural, *"eye"* is singular. This would mean that whatever the ephah represents, they share a single eye of sorts. This could be the establishment of the eye of the enemy that Jesus is to destroy.

In considering what the ephah might represent, we discover that the text is not completely clear who is being referred to as "their". The most accepted answer is "their" is referring to the sinners back in the vision of the scroll. This conclusion is reached by going backwards through the text from "their" to discover the subject. Normally, the first subject that can fit is the correct one.

---

[56] https://www.bible.com/notes/7052258

CHAPTER 5

Here, however, it is a bit difficult to know for sure because we are within a completely new vision. Within this vision, the only subject that has been addressed is the ephah itself. If *"their"* is referring to the ephah, then it would seem to say there are multiple objects throughout the earth that resemble this ephah. If *"their"* is referring to the sinners in the previous vision, then the spiritual or metaphorical resemblance of the sinners is that of the ephah. That is, of course, if we are to go with the resemblance translation instead of the eye translation. Either way, there is a cryptic meaning that seems to point to the same thing. All we need to do is discover what an ephah actually is.

The word "ephah" comes from the Hebrew word *"eyphah"* meaning *"1 - a dry measure of quantity, equal to 3 seahs, 10 omers; the same as the liquid measure bath; (about 9 imperial gallons (40 l), rabbinical writings give sizes of one-half this amount) 2 - the receptacle for measuring or holding that amount"*.[57] We can think of this in terms of a cup or a gallon. Much how we would have a cup of flour or a gallon of milk, the same principal can be applied to the ephah. The cup of flour is in reference to the measurement and the container. The cup of flour is contained in a cup. The same goes for the gallon of milk. The gallon of milk is contained in a gallon. This seems to be what is

---

[57] "Hebrew Lexicon :: H374 (KJV)." Blue Letter Bible. Accessed 24 Nov, 2013. http://www.blueletterbible.org/lang/Lexicon/Lexicon.cfm?Strongs=H374&t=KJV

expressed in the word "ephah". It is the name of the measurement and of the container. Since this is a vision that Zechariah is having, it would be referring to the container instead of the measurement.

Taking even a quick glance at the physical appearance of an ephah (Figure 7) should bring about new meaning to the idea of this being *"their resemblance"*, or even *"their eye"*.[58] If it is meant to be *"their resemblance"* and is referring to the ephah itself, what does this ephah resemble? The striking resemblance of the ephah to many of the UFOs that are being witnessed and reported today stands out immediately. If it is meant as *"their resemblance"* and is referring back to the sinners of the flying scroll vision, then the more spiritual or metaphoric resemblance would be addressed. What do the pilots of these certain chariots promulgate?

Figure 7- Picture of an Ephah

As is addressed by researchers and authors such as L.A. Marzulli, S. Douglas Woodward, and many others, the pilots of certain UFOs today are the carriers of a lie which states we were created by extraterrestrials and not by God. This is sometimes referred to as the Alien Gospel. In this view, the promulgators of

---

[58] Screencap taken from Quest4Truth

the lie are stealing the faith of many and stealing many out of the Church while cursing God. We seem to have references to both of the sins that are dealt with in the flying scroll vision.

If it is meant as *"their eye"* and is referring back to the sinners of the flying scroll vision, this could fit as well. The establishment of the eye of the enemy in the last days will be built upon a foundation of false doctrine. The false doctrine that causes the great apostasy, in all likelihood, will be or have something to do with the Alien Gospel. If it is meant as *"their eye"* and is referring to the ephah itself, then it is plain and simple in meaning. This ephah in the air, this UFO of sorts, is a representation of the eye of the enemy. This is how they watch, study, and learn the best ways to deceive us. Whichever of these four interpretations is correct, they all lead back to the same thing. They all point to the Alien Gospel.

We can find further evidence to support this by looking at the rest of the vision.

"And, behold, there was lifted up a talent of lead: and this is a woman that sitteth in the midst of the ephah

Zechariah 5:7

The word for *"talent"* refers to a weight and a circular shape.[59] Also, the word for *"sitteth"* denotes the act of dwelling or residing. This woman was not just sitting inside of the ephah. The woman dwelt there. The ephah is the woman's residence. This could mean that her whole drive or motivation is contained in what she promulgates with this ephah. This could also have reference to the fall of the angels who lost their first estate and proper residence. The fallen angels no longer have a home in Heaven, but now seem to reside somewhere in the air, the space between Heaven and Earth, or what is sometimes referred to as the Second Heaven.

"And he said, This is wickedness. And he cast it into the midst of the ephah; and he cast the weight of lead upon the mouth thereof."

Zechariah 5:8

The name of the woman is Wickedness. Another word for this can be Lawlessness and can be compared with the whore of Babylon, as we will soon see. After identifying the woman, we discover the purpose for the talent of lead. This heavy, circular piece of lead was being used as a lid to contain the woman inside the ephah. We

---

[59] "Hebrew Lexicon :: H3603 (KJV)." Blue Letter Bible. Accessed 24 Nov, 2013.
http://www.blueletterbible.org/lang/Lexicon/Lexicon.cfm?Strongs=H3603&t=KJV

discover the reason in the next three verses, which are the last three of the chapter and the end of the vision of the ephah.

5:9 Then lifted I up mine eyes, and looked, and, behold, there came out two women, and the wind was in their wings; for they had wings like the wings of a stork: and they lifted up the ephah between the earth and the heaven.

5:10 Then said I to the angel that talked with me, Whither do these bear the ephah?

5:11 And he said unto me, To build it an house in the land of Shinar: and it shall be established, and set there upon her own base.

Zechariah 5:9-11

There is a lot to look at here. First we will discover what we can about the two women with the wings of storks.

What is first interesting to note is these spiritual beings lifted the ephah between the earth and the heaven. I would suggest that is representing where the fallen angels reside. What is also especially important to note is that these spiritual beings are women. Many times in scripture, when trying to convey spiritual ideas and principals, shadows of real life are used. One such example is using the idea of an adulterous woman as a shadow of idolatry, worshipping false gods, or following false doctrines. We see this in the book of Revelation when it refers to the whore of Babylon. The fact that these two spiritual beings are women could mean that they have some part in deceiving mankind away from God. This can be further shown by looking at their description.

We are told that the two women have the wings of storks. There are two main places in the Bible where we can find references to storks and what they could represent. Leviticus 11:19 and Deuteronomy 14:18 tells us that God considers the stork as an unclean bird. The stork was not kosher. It was not meant to be eaten. At times, God will use unclean animals to represent spiritual uncleanliness, sin, rebellion, and other things of that nature. This shows that these two women are not on the side of God but are in alliance with the enemy.

The two stork-women might be an evil shadow of the two witnesses of Revelation. In the Bible, a common pattern seems to be that for everything God has, Satan has an evil and inferior duplicate or shadow. These two women, as we will soon discover, play a very important role in the establishment of the enemy and their false doctrines. The two witnesses of God in the book of Revelation are sent to proclaim the truth and correct doctrine.

What is also interesting is that the eleventh chapter of the book of Revelation starts off by making references to the measurements of the temple. This is exactly how Zechariah 5 starts off with the flying scroll vision. First, before anything else, the measurements pointing back to the temple are described. After the measurements in Revelation 11, the very next thing discussed is God's two witnesses. In Zechariah 5, after the measurements are discussed, the next thing is the ephah vision with these two stork-women. They are a polar opposite of the two witnesses of God in every way. These two stork-women will play a part in the spiritual aspect of promulgating the lie that brings about the apostasy while the two witnesses of God will be trying to call back humanity with the truth.

Next, in possibly the most interesting verse of this entire chapter, we find out the true purpose of the ephah, the woman in the ephah, and the stork-women carrying the ephah. We learn that the two stork-women are taking the ephah *"To build it an house in the land of Shinar: and it shall be established, and set there upon her own base."* We have a reference to an establishment, such as what we looked at earlier concerning the establishment of the eye. We also have a reference to Shinar, which was where the tower of Babel, and later the city of Babylon, was built.

The Hebrew word used for *"build"* in this verse is not only referring to a physical act of constructing a dwelling, but also could refer to a rebuilding of a structure or even the building up of a family.[60] The rebuilding aspect could be a direct reference to the tower of Babel that is discussed in Genesis 11. This has all sorts

---

[60] "Hebrew Lexicon :: H1129 (KJV)." Blue Letter Bible. Accessed 24 Nov, 2013.
http://www.blueletterbible.org/lang/Lexicon/Lexicon.cfm?Strongs=H1129&t=KJV

of shadows tying back to Nimrod, the first one-world governmental and religious system, the false doctrines the people practiced, and even back to the idea of Nimrod himself attempting to contact the fallen angels and enter Heaven. The idea of the family could be in reference to a future genetic cohesion in which humanity and these fallen, extradimensional beings will create a type of hybrid race. For more information on this, I have gone into extensive detail concerning Nimrod and the Tower of Babel in my book *Disclosure*.[61, 62]

We also learn that this house or family that is to be built will have this ephah as its base. The ephah with the woman Wickedness will be the foundation of the building. This is where all of the false doctrines, idolatry, and worship of false gods will have its revival. It will originate here, in the land of Shinar, just as in Genesis with the Tower of Babel.

The Tower of Babel was the place of man's original collective rebellion against God. We can look at this as a prophetic shadow for what is to come in our future. Just as Nimrod attempted to reach into the heavens, enlist the fallen angels, and overthrow God, we may see mankind reach out into the heavens toward our supposed alien creators, enlist their help when they come to offer it, and strip God out of all human belief. At that

---

[61] Available at www.ministudyministry.com

[62] Also check out *The Shinar Directive: Preparing the Way for the Son of Perdition* by Dr. Michael Lake.

point, mankind won't have a use for God because the evidence supporting the Alien Gospel will be tangible and available to all. This is all speculation, of course, but this could be a prophecy of the coming great deception.

This woman in the ephah seems to be the ultimate spirit of false doctrine. This could be the same woman that is referred to as the whore of Babylon in Revelation 17 and 18. We are told in Revelation 17:15 that the woman sits on many waters, which seems to represent all peoples, nations, and tongues. This could be representing the worldwide deception. We also learn at the end of chapter 17 of Revelation that the whore is also a great city. This can relate back to the woman in the ephah. A house was built upon the base of the ephah containing the woman. Whether this is the literal location of this city or not is beside the point. Wherever it will manifest on Earth, this seems to act as the source of the deception.

Another intriguing verse relating to this is found in Revelation:

"And he cried mightily with a strong voice, saying, Babylon the great is fallen, is fallen, and is become the habitation of devils, and the hold of every foul spirit, and a cage of every unclean and hateful bird."

Revelation 18:2

This is a description of the fall of the city Babylon that was represented by the woman. We learn that it has become the habitation of devils and foul spirits. Next, we are given a peculiar description. We are told that it has become a cage of every unclean and hateful bird. We found out earlier that the stork is an unclean bird. It was the description of a stork that Zechariah attributed to the two women carrying the ephah. This could be a reference to the two stork-women. It could be saying the city and deception the stork-women were trying to implement has become their cage.

There is one more important shadow that should be addressed concerning the vision of the flying scroll and the vision of the ephah. In Leviticus 16, we read of the two goats that were to be used for atonement. We read that one goat was to be slaughtered while the other was to be abandoned in the wilderness for *"a scapegoat"*. The goat does not *become* a scapegoat. Rather, the goat is *for* a scapegoat. What is really interesting is that the word *"scapegoat"*, as used here, actually comes from the Hebrew word *"azazel"* which is a name that comes from the Book of Enoch.[63] As we touched on earlier, Azazel was one of the 200 watcher angels that fell from Heaven to mate with human women. This is the same event that is described in Genesis chapter six. In

---

[63] "Hebrew Lexicon :: H5799 (KJV)." Blue Letter Bible. Accessed 24 Nov, 2013.
http://www.blueletterbible.org/lang/Lexicon/Lexicon.cfm?Strongs=H5799&t=KJV

the book of Enoch, it is said that Azazel is the worst of all the 200 and, when God judged the fallen angels, all sin was ascribed to Azazel. This could be why the book of Leviticus describes one goat slaughtered for atonement and one goat abandoned in the wilderness for Azazel.

We can look at these two goats as shadows of the two visions in Zechariah chapter 5. The first goat was to be slaughtered for atonement. This is a shadow of the vision of the flying scroll. The flying scroll came to bring about judgment and cleanse the entire world of sin. What the first goat's job was for the people of Israel, the flying scroll's job is for the entire world. The second goat that was sent out to Azazel could be a shadow of the vision of the ephah. The goat was to be sent out into the wilderness to Azazel who, as recorded in the book of Enoch, was judged and buried somewhere in the wilderness until the time of the final judgment. When Azazel fell, he brought all sorts of deception to mankind that made them turn from God. That is exactly what we see with the woman in the ephah. She is buried, in a sense, in the wilderness and the establishment of the enemy is built upon her. The result of this could be the bringing about of all kinds of deceptions that revolve around a return of the fallen angels in physical form masquerading as our alien creators. We will look a bit more into Azazel and possible prophecies surrounding him in a later chapter. Now that we have looked at the scroll and the ephah, we can look into Zechariah's visions of the horses.

The Horses

I included more extensive information about Zechariah's horses in *Disclosure*. For this section, a brief review will suffice. In *Disclosure*, I showed how the horses of Zechariah 6 could be connected to the religion of Islam and a possible prophetic fulfillment. I explained the connection between the grisled/bay horses of Zechariah chapter 6 and the pale/green horse of Revelation chapter 6. I also showed that the horses of Zechariah were set out to fulfill the will of God while the horses of Revelation are set out to fulfill the will of the enemy. Taking the descriptions back to the original Hebrew and Greek languages, I explained the significance of the colors of the horses to show that the agents of the enemy are nothing more than an inferior duplicate of the agents of God.

We know from Zechariah that the horses of God were brought to the earth with Heavenly chariots. It is important to note that the horses are not described as pulling the chariots. The horses were *inside* the chariots. Whatever the proper interpretation and definition of these Heavenly chariots are, it would seem that the enemy has an evil and inferior duplicate, or shadow, of them as well. We see these in the form of extradimensional UFOs.

Since the horses Zechariah saw were brought to the earth with chariots, it would make sense that Satan will do something similar when the time of the pale/green horse comes. This might come in the form of a physical manifestation of the chariots of the enemy being portrayed as alien spacecraft. If Satan decides to, once again, steal an idea from God and twist it to suit his own desires, the pale/green horse of Revelation could be an example of the physical appearance of extradimensional craft and the promulgation of the Alien Gospel throughout the entire world. The pale/green horse could be signifying the great apostasy. The fourth seal of Revelation could be the arrival and worldwide acceptance of the coming great deception. At the very least, it could be a shadow pointing toward the end-time fulfillment of the falling away of the Church. Of course, this is only one possible interpretation.

War and Pestilence

On the other hand and setting aside the UFO interpretation aside for the moment, if the interpretation of the pale/green horse representing Islam proves to be correct, there are further developments that can be examined by looking at comparative passages:

"For nation shall rise against nation, and kingdom against kingdom: and there shall be famines, and pestilences, and earthquakes, in divers places."

Matthew 24:7

We see this theme in greater detail in the book of Revelation, specifically concerning the breaking of the fourth seal:

"And I looked, and behold a pale horse: and his name that sat on him was Death, and Hell followed with him. And power was given unto them over the fourth part of the earth, to kill with sword, and with hunger, and with death, and with the beasts of the earth."

Revelation 6:8

When we look at the full progression of prophetic events described in the book of Matthew and compare them with the seals of Revelation, we discover they all line up quite well. However, this type of exhaustive study is a bit outside our purposes here. For now, we will focus on two of these predictions: war and pestilence.

There is a lot that can be learned from looking at the original Greek of Revelation 6:8. As I stated earlier, it is possible the pale/green horse represents radicalized Islam. If this is true, the group known as ISIS (or ISIL) is probably the strongest candidate the world has seen to date for a possible fulfilment. This begs the question, are we seeing a direct fulfillment or are we seeing a birth pain? It is possible that ISIS is a shadow of a future fulfillment that will be far worse.

If the pale/green horse in Revelation 6:8 represents Islam, then we should expect that interpretation to follow the rest of the verse. Notice specifically there are two entities mentioned apart from the horse. There is a rider named Death and a follower named Hell. It also says that power was given to them (plural, meaning both entities) over a fourth of the earth. Lastly, we read they kill with the sword (war), hunger (famine), death, and beasts of the earth.

If the Islamic interpretation of the horse is correct, it is possible that ISIS may fulfill one of the entities, supported by the description of the killing by the sword and death. The other entity could represent pestilence. We can consider the recent Ebola outbreak as a possible fulfillment of this other rider. If it is not a direct fulfillment, it at least could be a shadow or birth pain.

We read that one of the ways these riders kill is with the beasts of the earth. It is possible that this could be referring to a delivery system for pestilence. The CDC website lists one of the causes of Ebola as such:

"People also can become sick with Ebola if they come into contact with infected wildlife or raw or undercooked meat (bushmeat) from an infected animal."[64]

This shows that Ebola can be passed to humans from wild animals. It is possible this is how the beasts of the earth are used to aid in the killing of a fourth of the world's population.

---

[64] http://wwwnc.cdc.gov/travel/notices/warning/ebola-liberia

It is also interesting to note the area of outbreak in West Africa compared against the religious beliefs of the same area (Figures 8 and 9). Consider the maps below:[65, 66]

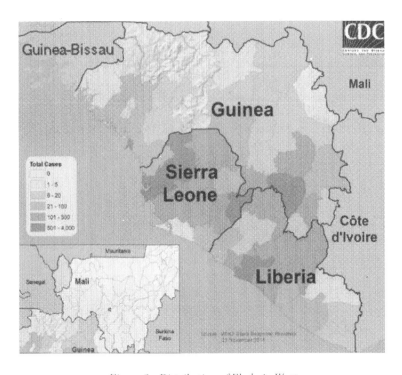

Figure 8 - Distribution of Ebola in West Africa

---

[65]   http://www.cdc.gov/vhf/ebola/outbreaks/2014-west-africa/distribution-map.html

[66] http://en.wikipedia.org/wiki/Religion_in_Africa

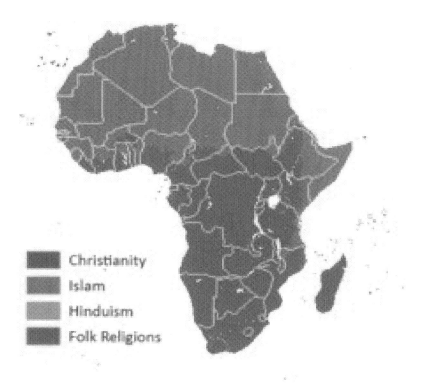

Figure 9 - Religion in Africa

The interesting thing to notice is that much of the outbreak is in the Islamic part of the country, but also that the initial outbreak took place in Sierra Leone and Liberia. According to Wikipedia, Sierra Leone is a majorly Islamic territory whereas Liberia is majorly Christian.

The two faiths of Islam and Christianity could not be further apart in theology. Due to this fact, much contention ensues. This fact could be a representation of the rider on the horse responsible for death by the sword.

If Islam, ISIS, and Ebola are the fulfillment of the horse, rider, and follower of Revelation 6:8, then we can expect each aspect to grow exponentially and get far worse in the very near future. If it is a birth pain, then we should expect to see them fizzle out and be replaced by something far more horrific. In the case that it is a birth pain, we may have a bit more time before things become extreme, but it is only a delay of the inevitable. In either event and even though all the possible interpretations we looked at throughout this chapter are speculative, we should be preparing now while we are still able to do so. After all, it is far better to be needlessly prepared than to be regretfully unprepared.

Interview with Sharon K. Gilbert

Sharon K. Gilbert is the author of *Ebola and the Fourth Horseman of the Apocalypse*. She has studied Bible prophecy for over 50 years and uses her background in molecular biology to show how Ebola might be mentioned in the book of Revelation. She also cohosts PID Radio with her husband Derek. In my humble opinion, there is nobody better suited to provide information concerning this topic. A special thanks goes out to

CHAPTER 5

Sharon for taking the time to contribute to the book by taking part in an interview.

*   *   *

JOSH PECK: What connections are there between Ebola and the fourth seal of Revelation?

SHARON GILBERT: The Fourth Horseman is all about pestilence and disease. If you look at his description, you'll see that he is the only NAMED rider of the four. I contend that these four horsemen are supernatural entities given permission by God to transform humanity into a One World Order. This has been the dream of geopoliticians for decades—in fact, some might say for millennia. The named rider on the pale green horse is called 'Thanatos'. This is the name of a primordial god who served as henchman to Hades. Note that it is Hades who follows along with Thanatos. These two serve the same purpose: to harvest unsaved humans and toss them into hell. Thanatos has a twin brother named Hypnos who transports saved humans to heaven or 'Abraham's Bosom'. Hypnos is a gentle 'reaper', putting humans to sleep (note that Paul refers to dead saints as 'sleeping'). Thanatos is not gentle. He brings 'therion' as his weapon along with a rhomphaia (the scythe). Therion is Greek for small or tiny beasts as well as a reference to large beasts, but coupled with the reference to pestilence, I believe that Thanatos and Hades will bring a worldwide pandemic, which could be Ebola but could also be a new, engineered disease. *Ordo ab Chao*, Order out of Chaos is the watch phrase for those in power who seek to transform the Earth into One Governed Body. A worldwide pandemic would serve their purposes by eliminating large portions of the population (Thanatos is given power to kill 25% of humanity), and it would pave the way for strict controls over commerce and travel. As we've seen with Ebola's small footprint in the West (US and Europe), it won't take much to trigger a major shift in policy.

JOSH PECK: Is there a possibility that Ebola shows up in other Bible prophecies?

SHARON GILBERT: As mentioned above, Ebola may be one type of 'therion' employed by Thanatos. The English word 'pestilence' occurs 47 times in the KJV translation, and it nearly always refers to judgment upon either Israel or the surrounding nations. Psalm 91 has an interesting reference to pestilence. This Psalm speaks to all who believe in Him now, but particularly to those who will live during the time of the Riders, that is the final seven years of Daniel's prophecy of Seventy Weeks (i.e. the Tribulation Week):

CHAPTER 5

1. *He who dwells in the shelter of the Most High will abide in the shadow of the Almighty.*

2. *I will say to the Lord,* **"My refuge and my fortress, my God, in whom I trust."**

3. *For* **he will deliver you from the snare of the fowler and from the deadly pestilence.**

4. *He* **will cover you with his pinions, and under his wings you will find refuge;** *his faithfulness is a shield and buckler.*

5. **You will not fear the terror of the night, nor the arrow that flies by day,**

6. **nor the pestilence that stalks in darkness, nor the destruction that wastes at noonday.**

Psalm 91: 1-6 [emphases added]

I've emphasized several of these phrases. Remember how Jesus wept before entering Jerusalem just before the final few days of His mortal life? He told how He longed to gather them all beneath His 'wings' (pinions) as a hen would gather her chicks to protect them, but that 'they would not'. During the Tribulation period, Christ will supernaturally protect His own—both Messianic Jews and Christians, for all who trust in Him are of the same 'body'. Notice the phrase that personifies pestilence, saying that it 'stalks in darkness'. Perhaps this is a reference to our limited understanding even now of how viruses emerge. They appear to come out of nowhere. The Ebola virus and her sisters Marburg and Cuevavirus seemed to come out of nowhere in the Congo region of Africa in the 1970s. Hantavirus, a cousin, emerged during the Korean War. In fact, it might be said that war and famine preceded their emergence, for conflict had left Congo's people impoverished and physically weak. The Four Riders are permitted to ride only when He commands it---but I believe that they've been saddled up for a long time, and their hellish steeds champ at the bit to go forth.

JOSH PECK: What are some things about Ebola that everyone needs to know?

SHARON GILBERT: First of all, Ebola is highly contagious and it can be spread via aerosolized droplets. Early in the outbreak, both the CDC and the World Health Organization (WHO) repeatedly told reporters that the disease was not airborne, but this language is deceptive. While it is NOT truly airborne in the way Smallpox is (a viral particle that can ride on air currents like smoke), Ebola does spread via coughs and sneezes, so it is possible to 'catch it' without touching bodily fluids directly.

Secondly, Ebola needn't be a death sentence. Researchers have been using this outbreak in West Africa to try a variety of methods to curtail the disease, and two methods have been repeatedly helpful. One is to infuse the patient as soon as possible with blood plasma from a survivor, making use of preprogrammed B-cells and T-cells. All patients who have received this therapy early have survived. Also, doctors have realized that hydration plays a major role in survival. Patients often die from hypovolemic shock (not enough blood), so IV therapy with a sugar/electrolyte solution has shown promise—especially when the patient is placed into an 'induced coma', which slows the body's metabolism and allows therapy to catch up with the virus.

Thirdly, while Ebola may 'go away' this year, it will always lurk in the shadows. One day, a pandemic will arise because God has said it would, so Christians must prepare their homes and their hearts by building up a storehouse that equips us to serve as an ad hoc hospital if necessary. My book lists many ways to do this, and it includes a great deal of information about how Ebola infects a patient and how best to prepare a 'sick room', etc. in your home.

JOSH PECK: Ebola doesn't seem to be reported on as much as it used to; is this because infection is declining or are there other reasons for the lack of coverage?

SHARON GILBRT: No, Ebola infections are slowing in West Africa, praise the Lord. We must rejoice for that! I do suspect however, mainstream news media have been told to keep reporting to a minimum. Recently, reporter Sharyl Attkisson asked the CDC just how many Ebola patients were being 'tracked' in the United

States.[67] Attkisson told Howard Kurtz on Media Buzz that the CDC is hiding suspected cases from the American public:

"Infectious disease experts remain very concerned about the disease… A lot of the media coverage has gone from overtime to almost nothing since the administration has appointed an Ebola czar. And I don't think that's any accident. That's a strategy… ***I called CDC not long ago and said, "How many active cases are being monitored in the United States of Ebola?" And they said, "1,400." And I said, "Where is that on your website, these updates?" And they said, "We're not putting it on the web."*** *So I think there's an effort to control the message and tamp it down. This is public information we have a right to and I think the media should not hype it but cover it."* [emphasis added]

This story broke in December just before Christmas. I believe that Ron Klain, appointed as 'Ebola Czar' by President Obama, sent orders to the MSM and the CDC to keep a lid on reports so that the Christmas shopping season would not be impacted negatively. If people fear public places because of Ebola, then they might not shop, right? Money is king, because money is the key to power. At that time, most people in America believed that only a handful of 'cases' existed. One has to wonder how many military men and women who have returned from their mission to West Africa have

---

[67]   http://www.thegatewaypundit.com/2014/12/sharyl-attkisson-cdc-is-tracking-1400-possible-ebola-cases-in-us-today-video/):

been exposed. Recently, a soldier who had just returned from WA was found dead, and we've been told that his death had nothing to do with Ebola. There have been numerous 'mystery deaths' since Ebola's emergence in WA that show Ebola symptoms and signs, but again and again we are told "there is nothing to see here".

JOSH PECK: What can people do to prepare for a potential outbreak?

SHARON GILBERT: As I mentioned earlier, every Christian with the funds to do so (and the directing by the Holy Spirit) can and should prepare his/her home to become an ad hoc hospital. Begin now to purchase PPEs (Personal Protective Equipment) consisting of an impermeable outer garment, mask, hood, and gloves—perhaps even booties. These can be bought at online resources such as Amazon. Stock your home with plastic sheeting, inexpensive towels and sheets, a cot, medical supplies such as bandages, iodine or betadine, extra water and food, gauze masks, and Bibles. Print Bibles will be needed because it is very likely that the Internet and perhaps even electricity will 'go down' one day, and panicked people who begin to realize that 'those Christians were right!' will want to read His word. Even if the rapture takes us, our deserted homes can serve as a haven where people can find comfort both physically and spiritually.

It's so easy in our culture to trust in 'society' to provide all our needs. Those who work with evil entities (demons and fallen angels) to plan a New World Order will use chaos to achieve their goals, and the Lord will permit this, but only in HIS timing. Our society will break down, and we will be left only with a choice: Serve God or Serve the AntiChrist. Let us prepare our homes to be witness to Him.

*   *   *

Make sure to check out *Ebola and the Fourth Horseman of the Apocalypse* by Sharon K. Gilbert.[68] Visit www.SharonKGilbert.com to find out more about Sharon and her ministry. Also visit www.PIDRadio.com to check out PID Radio, hosted by Derek and Sharon Gilbert.

---

[68]   Available at http://www.amazon.com/Fourth-Horseman-Apocalypse-Sharon-Gilbert/dp/0990497445   and http://www.survivormall.com/ProductDetails.asp?ProductCode=EbolaSO

Unfolding Cherubim

Ezekiel's Vision

The first chapter of the book of Ezekiel is especially fascinating and truly mind-bending. Throughout the entire book, the overall meanings and purposes of the vision are explained, however there are many aspects that are not. In the past, many people have offered their own ideas and conclusions. I myself have attempted this (to a certain lesser degree than most) in *Disclosure*. Since that time, further study and research has provoked me to take another look at Ezekiel's vision.

Extradimensional Unfolding

Before we get into what Ezekiel actually saw, a certain framework is necessary. This framework may seem completely irrelevant at first, but will be important later on. We need to establish an understanding in the idea of "unfolding" to help visualize higher dimensions.

Extradimensional unfolding is something I tackle in full in my book *Quantum Creation* but for our purposes here, a basic understanding will suffice.[69] The idea is to think of how something from a higher dimension of space could describe, represent, or explain itself to something from a lower dimension of space. One tactic is that of unfolding. To help explain this, here is an excerpt from chapter three of *Quantum Creation*:

In his book "Hyperspace: A Scientific Odyssey through Parallel Universes, Time Warps, and the 10th Dimension", physicist Michio Kaku gives an example of a way to explain a three-dimensional object in two-dimensional understanding. He shows how you can unfold a cube into a two-dimensional shape (Figure 10).
Interestingly enough, this shape is that of a cross.

Figure 10 - A Cube Unfolding into a 2-dimensional Shape

The idea is, since a cube is essentially six two-dimensional planes

---

[69] *Quantum Creation* is available at www.ministudyministry.com

folded together in three-dimensional space, you can unfold the cube to show what it would look like in two dimensions. While this idea of unfolding does not result in quite as much information-loss as a projection, it is still not a perfect device. Since there is no perfect device, if you wanted to explain a cube to Flatlanders [hypothetical beings consisting of only two spatial dimensions], this is one of the methods you could use.

We can think of this in terms of three and four spatial dimensions. If we want to try and understand a hypercube [a cube consisting of four spatial dimensions instead of three], we can, in

a sense, "unfold" the hypercube into three spatial dimensions. The result is what is known as a "tesseract" (Figure 11). Just as a cube is made of six squares, a tesseract is made of eight cubes. Though this is not a perfect device to aid in visualizing a hypercube, it can at least translate a hypercube into dimensions we can perceive.

Figure 11 - The Unfolding of a Hypercube is called a Tesseract

What is also interesting about a tesseract is that it would not unfold at one-dimensional hinges like a cube does. There is a digression of dimensions when unfolding into lower dimensions. To unfold a three-dimensional cube into two-dimensional space, it must be unfolded along one-dimensional hinges (or lines). Similarly, to unfold a four-

dimensional hypercube into three-dimensional space, it must be unfolded along two-dimensional planes (Figure 12).

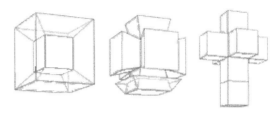

Imagine what it would look like to a Flatlander if you were to fold the two-dimensional cross back up into a cube.

Figure 12 - The Progression of Unfolding from 4 Spatial Dimensions to 3

From the perspective of the Flatlander, he would only see the two-dimensional squares disappear as they are folded up into the third spatial dimension. Similarly, if a tesseract were to be folded back up into a hypercube, we would only see the cubes disappear as they are folded up into the fourth spatial dimension.

Now imagine what would happen if the Flatlander were inside the two-dimensional cross as it is being folded up into the third dimension. Since the Flatlander has no concept of the third spatial dimension, the Flatlander would not notice anything unusual at first. He would move along the squares just as he did before the folding happened. As he moves from square to square, however, he would soon realize the squares are repeating. Upon realizing this, he would make the discovery that he is trapped. Another interesting hypothetical situation would be if the Flatlander entered the cube after it was folded up. From his perspective, the cube would look only like a common square. Upon entering, however, he would realize the inside appears much larger than the outside and there are multiple squares. Upon moving from square to square, it would be easy for the Flatlander to become confused and trapped within the cube.

Keeping this idea of unfolding in mind, we might be able to discover what exactly Ezekiel was attempting to describe.

Possible Interpretations

Now we can begin to look at the actual vision Ezekiel experienced. Probably the best way to do this is to examine the described vision in sections and examine each one independently.

"And I looked, and, behold, a whirlwind came out of the north, a great cloud, and a fire infolding itself, and a brightness was about it, and out of the midst thereof as the colour of amber, out of the midst of the fire."

Ezekiel 1:4

In one of many conversations I have had with my good friend Jim Wilhelmsen, author of *Beyond Science Fiction*, he offered an interesting theory concerning this whirlwind.[70] He mentioned how most people would picture in their minds something like a tornado when reading this passage. He then suggested thinking of it in

---

[70] www.echoesofenoch.com

terms of an upside-down tornado or a tornado tipped on its side, thereby describing something looking more like a vortex or a wormhole, not unlike the documented Norway Spiral of 2009 (Figure 13). A biblical connection to this idea is the description of Elijah being taken up in a whirlwind (2 Kings

Figure 13 - The Norway Spiral

2:11). I found this to be especially intriguing when considering that Ezekiel describes something from outside our three-spatial-dimensional reality coming through and out of the whirlwind.

"Also out of the midst thereof came the likeness of four living creatures. And this was their appearance; they had the likeness of a man."

Ezekiel 1:5

This tells us that four beings came out from the center of the whirlwind. These beings are described as being alive and having the likeness of a man, most likely signifying their basic shape was humanoid in appearance, at least from Ezekiel's three-dimensional perspective. That said, these beings do seem to be bodily connected together in some way as one living "construct" (for lack of better term). We will see this in later verses, but for now, notice specifically the text states *"They* (plural) *had the likeness of a man* (singular). The four were connected together as one.

"And every one had four faces, and every one had four wings."

Ezekiel 1:6

There have been many artistic attempts to express what this might look like. The main thing to recognize is the text says *"every one had"*, meaning this is a description of each of the four beings; it is not a description of the connected group as a whole. This means if you were to consider the appearance of only one of the beings disconnected from the other three, it would have four faces and four wings. If every one of the four being had four faces, that would mean the entire living construct would have sixteen faces in total (four face for each of the four beings; 4x4=16). This, of course, conflicts a bit with traditional depictions, but given the language of the text, I believe this is a reasonable assumption.

"And their feet were straight feet; and the sole of their feet was like the sole of a calf's foot: and they sparkled like the colour of burnished brass."

Ezekiel 1:7

This shows one way in which these living beings are connected together. We can first notice that it uses the plural word *"feet"*, yet uses the singular word *"sole"*. It says *"the sole* (singular) *of their feet* (plural) *was like the sole of a calf's foot* (singular). Interestingly, the Hebrew word used here for *"feet"* is *"kaph"* and can include the leg. This seems to be conveying the idea that the tops of the beings' legs start out separate, but as they extend down, at some point they meld or converge into one until, by the time you get to the very bottom, they all share a single sole.

"And they had the hands of a man under their wings on their four sides; and they four had their faces and their wings."

Ezekiel 1:8

This one is pretty straight-forward. Ezekiel is telling us that under the wings, the beings had hands like that of a man. The text states *"they* (plural*) had the hands* (plural) *of a man* (singular)". A single man possesses two hands. The text seems to apply that each being had two hands: one under each wing. This was found on all four sides, bringing the total number of hands to eight. Ezekiel then reaffirms what he already explained by reminding us that they each of the four had multiple faces and wings. Next, Ezekiel gives one of the most profound descriptions of one of the most interesting aspects of this entire vision.

"Their wings were joined one to another; they turned not when they went; they went every one straight forward."

Ezekiel 1:9

This is telling us that each wing was connected to the wing next to it. The common depiction shows these wings connected only at the tips, but Ezekiel's description doesn't seem to convey that idea. The Hebrew word for *"joined"* used here is *"chabar"* and means *"unite, join, bind together, be joined, be coupled"* among other things describing the same idea. It seems the wings were not merely joined at the tips, but rather were joined in full. The language seems to imply that every part of each wing was united, melded, or fused together with the wing next to it. It seems the same type of fusing together that was described with the legs is the same as we see with the wings. This is further supported by Ezekiel saying *they turned not when they went; they went every one straight forward.* Since they were fused together at the feet and the wings and since each had four faces, whatever direction this living structure decided to move, it would be considered as straight forward from the perspective of the beings.

One absolutely phenomenal thing to consider is the idea of the tesseract we discussed earlier. If we can try and imagine what this fusion of these beings would look like, we can notice it would have the same basic structure as a tesseract. I searched long and wide across the internet for an adequate image to illustrate this, but alas, I could find nothing representing this in all important aspects. I did, however, find a couple of images that come somewhat close, at least to the point that they should help in visualizing the similar shape of the tesseract in regards to the fused beings.

The first image (Figure 14) comes somewhat close to what Ezekiel is trying to describe, at least in my humble opinion. The problem is, however, it is difficult to make out the main image from the background. There are also inconsistencies between this image and Ezekiel's description. For example, Ezekiel describes each of the four living creatures as having four faces (bringing the total number of faces to sixteen, as we discussed

Figure 14 - One Depiction of Ezekiel's Vision

in our examination of Ezekiel 1:6). Also, Ezekiel describes each living creature as fused to the other three by leg and wing. The image presented here is a cropped section of a larger depiction which shows three more of these beings, all separate. There is scriptural evidence we looked at showing this is most likely not the case.

The next image we can look at (Figure 15) comes a little closer to at least showing the basic structure of the fused beings and how similar it is to that of a tesseract. There are clearly problems with other aspects of this depiction when compared against the description Ezekiel provides, but many of those inconsistencies are obvious and probably do not require

Figure 15 - Another Depiction of Ezekiel's Vision

to be commented on in full here. The main thing to notice is the similarity to a tesseract that the basic overall shape depicted here conveys.

The reason I believe this is so important to realize becomes clearer when we remember what a tesseract actually is. Remember, a tesseract is the three-dimensional unfolding of a hypercube. A hypercube is a cube that consists of four spatial dimensions instead of three. Now, imagine unfolding a four-dimensional hypercube into a three-dimension tesseract, then unfolding that same three dimensional tesseract into a two-dimensional representation. Such a thing is difficult to imagine, but it would involve a lot of fusing and melding of the squares as they would have to take up the same space. That is why I believe Ezekiel saw something that originates from an even higher dimension than the fourth-spatial. That could be why, from Ezekiel's three-dimensional perspective, he saw a strange fusing and melding of the beings. What Ezekiel saw seems to be the result of the literal unfolding of higher-dimensional beings into three spatial dimensions. Ezekiel saw something truly amazing and he clearly described it to the best of his ability.

The Living Faces

The next thing Ezekiel describes is the faces of the living beings.

"As for the likeness of their faces, they four had the face of a man, and the face of a lion, on the right side: and they four had the face of an ox on the left side; they four also had the face of an eagle."

Ezekiel 1:10

This is a very interesting description and when we look deeply into the text, we see it is quite different than what is usually depicted artistically. In most artistic expressions, these four faces are shown to each be on a separate side: one on the left, one on the right, one in back, and one in front. However, notice what the text actually says. First, it says *they four had*, again meaning this is one common description of each of the four beings. Each one of the four beings has four faces, for a total of sixteen faces altogether.

CHAPTER 6

Next, notice it says *they four had the face of a man, and the face of a lion, on the right side:* signifying that the face of the lion and the face of the man were *both* on the right side. I believe it is entirely possible that this these two faces are actually split in the middle, thus creating a bisection of the head with the half-face of the lion on the left side and the half-face of the man on the right. As the late author and researcher David Flynn pointed out, this is seen later in the book of Ezekiel:[71]

[18] And it was made with cherubims and palm trees, so that a palm tree was between a cherub and a cherub; and every cherub had two faces;

[19] So that the face of a man was toward the palm tree on the one side, and the face of a young lion toward the palm tree on the other side: it was made through all the house round about.

Ezekiel 41:18-19

This is quite similar to the description of the face on Mars. Authors and researchers such as Mike Bara, Richard Hoagland, and David Flynn have done extensive work with interpreting the meaning of the face. One theory states the structure actually portrays two faces, one of a man and one of a lion, bisected and fused together

---

[71] http://www.mt.net/~watcher/newun.html

Figure 16 - The Face on Mars with a Bisected Facial Overlay

(Figure 16). For more information on this, I highly recommend *Cydonia: The Secret Chronicles of Mars* by David E. Flynn.

Next in Ezekiel's account, it says *they four had the face of an ox on the left side*; showing that the face of the ox was the only face on the left side. Lastly, it says *they four also had the face of an eagle*. What is interesting is the eagle is not given a side at all. For the eagle to have neither been on the right nor the left side, it must have been in the middle. Though simplistic, I believe the illustration below (Figure 17) to be an accurate example of a bird's-eye view of what is being described.

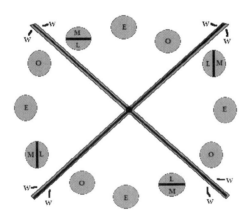

W - Wing, M - Man, L - Lion, E - Eagle, O - Ox

Figure 17 - A Bird's-Eye View showing the Faces of Ezekiel's Vision

As we can see here, each being has two outstretched wings, signified by black lines, which are both fused with the wings of the beings next to them, signified by the shading within the wings (keep in mind that each being actually has four wings, but Ezekiel 1:11 states two of the four wings of each being are covering its body which would not be seen in a bird's-eye view such as this). The bisected faces of the lion and man are on the right, the face of the ox is on the left side, and the face of the eagle is in the middle. This may fall a bit outside of traditional depictions of the four living beings, but given the scriptural evidence, it is my humble opinion that this is a fair assumption.

A New Possibility of Interpreting the Faces

In researching for my book, *Quantum Creation,* I often wondered if the faces of these creatures could somehow be symbolizing dimensions of space. I was presented with evidence showing the ox could represent the first dimension (the x axis). An ox is generally referred to as a domesticated animal in the Bible. When an ox is used to plow a field today, for example, it generally must walk in the one direction it is allowed. Also, as Mark Flynn points out in *Forbidden Secrets of the Labyrinth* and his blog on the Ox Circuit:

"The threshing floor in ancient times was a flat, circular area of smooth rock where an ox or a team of oxen would loosen wheat

grain from the hard, outer chaff. The method is still used today in places where modern machinery is not available. [72] (Figure 18)

To the perspective of the ox, it would be walking in one direction continually. The eternal, never-ending line that creates the circle could be a representation of the first dimension.

Figure 18 - The Ancient Threshing Floor

The lion could represent the second dimension. Since lions are wild in nature and not referred to as domesticated, a lion would have free reign to roam in two dimensions (the x and y axes); a lion can roam along the ground anywhere it chooses. The eagle, having the ability of flight, would be free to travel through the air and thus all three spatial dimensions (the x, y, and z axes). Man, having a living soul and thus a spiritual component, could be a representation of the fourth spatial dimension which, as I show in *Quantum Creation*, is synonymous with the spirit world: at the very least, the part of the spirit world that coincides and sometimes bleeds into our own.

The main problem I had was between the lion and the man. My concern was the lion might actually represent the fourth spatial

---

[72] http://www.markaflynn.com/meaning/the-revealing/the-ox-circuit/

dimension. I considered this because the lion is used in reference to Jesus Christ. A good example of this is Revelation 5:5 where Jesus Christ is called the lion of the tribe of Judah. This actually happens in Heaven, a place outside of the three spatial dimensions of our physical reality. Also, Satan is referred to as as *a roaring lion, seeking whom he may devour* (1 Peter 5:8). As I postulate in *Quantum Creation*, it is possible that when the rebellious angels fell, they may have fallen to the fourth spatial dimension. I also show several reasons why I believe Jesus Christ had access to the fourth spatial dimension after His resurrection. For these reasons, I wondered if perhaps the face of the lion was referencing the fourth spatial dimension and the face of the man was representing the second spatial dimension (man has free reign to walk in any direction on the face of the earth but lacks the natural ability of flight).

When I looked closer at Ezekiel's description, I realized that the face of the lion and the face of the man are most likely interchangeable. Both are bisected and located on the right side. This might show that both could have the ability to represent either the second or the fourth spatial dimension. This was the further evidence I needed to be comfortable in writing about the possibility of the four faces representing spatial dimensions.

Dimensional Cycles

Something else interesting that came up was a connection to Hebrew word pictures (another topic Mark Flynn talks about in *Forbidden Secrets of the Labyrinth*) and how the Aleph (the first letter of the ancient Hebrew alphabet) looked like an ox. Since the ox represents the first letter of the Hebrew alphabet, it could be further evidence to show that the ox also represents the first spatial dimension in Ezekiel's vision. Upon further research, I discovered something that could provide an answer to the location of the other dimensions within scripture.

In *Quantum Creation,* I describe the possibility of 12 dimensions making up the total construct of God's creation. These dimensions would be 10 of space (or spatial), 1 of time (or temporal), and 1 zeroth (or foundational). As I describe in full detail in *Quantum Creation,* modern M-theory states there are 11 dimensions (ten of space and one of time). There is also an idea of something called a "zeroth" dimension. Not every theoretical physicist adheres to this, but the basic idea is that if the first dimension is described as a line between two points, the zeroth dimension would be the place a single point would reside. To those who subscribe to the idea, it is seen as a foundation for all other dimensions. As I describe in *Quantum Creation,* the number 12 has all sorts of amazing connections regarding divine order within the texts of the Bible, but to go too deeply into detail concerning that would go a bit outside of our purposes here.

CHAPTER 6

To explain the cycle possibility, envision the four living creatures connected in the following way: imagine the starting point is the ox, then imagine a line going from the ox to the man (the lion and man are interchangeable, but for the sake of this thought exercise, we will just say the man represents the second spatial dimension). Next, imagine the line extending from the man to the eagle, then from the eagle to the lion. Now we have a bit of a dilemma. If the line connects back to the ox, then we are back to the first spatial dimension. But, what if the ox can change into something that represents the fifth spatial dimension? Consider a passage when Ezekiel later describes the four living creatures again:

"And every one had four faces: the first face was the face of a cherub, and the second face was the face of a man, and the third the face of a lion, and the fourth the face of an eagle."

Ezekiel 10:14

Here we can see that the face of the ox has been replaced by the face of a cherub. Even more, as we discussed earlier, the angels Ezekiel saw were most likely of the fifth spatial dimension (or higher) rather than the fourth due to the melding/fusing that signifies a type of double-unfolding between two lower dimensions. As we can see, the cycle continues, this time with the line connecting to the cherub (5th dimension) to the man (6th dimension and, interestingly enough, the number 6 is the biblical number of man), to the lion (7th dimension, having all sorts of implications, such as in the book of Revelation, especially if the lion represents Jesus), to the eagle (8th dimension). Yet, is this where is ends?

We see these beings show up again in the book of Revelation:

"And the first beast was like a lion, and the second beast like a calf, and the third beast had a face as a man, and the fourth beast was like a flying eagle."

Revelation 4:7

Since this scene is set in Heaven, outside of John's usual three dimensions of space, the cycles continue again and this time the line goes even higher. The line from the second mention of the eagle (8th dimension) would connect with the lion (9th dimension) to the calf, or what could be considered as a repeat of the ox (10th dimension) to the man (11th dimension) and finally to the eagle (12th dimension). It is interesting to note that this line cycles around three times in total. This could be a representation of God as Father, Son, and Holy Spirit.

Another way to visualize this whole cycle idea is that of an upward spiral. The spiral itself would consist of three revolutions. Keep in mind, this is only a thought exercise. In reality, the spiral would not be moving "up", as in regards to the z axis in three-dimensional space. Just as the first, second, and third dimensions exist within the same spatial reality, I believe it would be the same for the rest of the dimensions. The only difference is we can't actually see them. However, as long as we keep in mind we are not talking about a literal spatial movement in the upward direction as defined by the z axis, we can think of an upward spiral as a way to at least understand the concept of this cycle of dimensions.

The Revelation Connection

On last thing I will note is the difference in description of the four beasts of Revelation and the four beings of Ezekiel. In the book of Ezekiel, each time he describes the beings, he notices they are fused/melded together. We can recognize this as an unfolding of a higher-dimensional being into a lower spatial dimension as Ezekiel was seeing this from his three-spatial-dimensional environment. John, however, was able to see these beings (referred to as "beasts" in Revelation) in their higher-spatial-dimensional environment: the throne room in Heaven. John wasn't even sure if he was inside or outside of his body while all of this was going on so it is unclear if he was still subject to his own three-spatial-dimensional visual perception or not. Regardless, he still had to describe something that was witnessed in a higher spatial dimension to the rest of us who are of a perception limited to three spatial dimensions. That being the case, John was able to get a clearer view of the true appearance of these beings. That is why they were separate and not fused or melded together. John was not seeing the mere unfolding of these beings; John was seeing these beings as they really are, at least to the capacity his perception at the time allowed.

Living Extradimensional Vehicles

An Unpopular Theory

There is a very interesting, albeit unpopular, theory within the study of UFOs and extradimensional craft. The theory states that UFOs are not mechanical at all, but are actually biological. This theory sees UFOs as actual living, biological entities. What we see as a metallic craft is nothing more than a body for the consciousness or spirit inside.

The more popular version of this theory states that UFOs could be part biological and part mechanical. The idea is that a race of super-intelligent extraterrestrials have found a way to meld living material with nonliving physical components. The theory that states it is *all* biological, however, is less recognized as a viable explanation.

As we have seen in the first part of Ezekiel's account, the idea that an extradimensional craft is alive is really not a new concept at all. Ezekiel described the chariot of the throne of God as being made of living entities. This is even spoken about in the book of Psalms:

"And he rode upon a cherub, and did fly: yea, he did fly upon the wings of the wind."

Psalm 18:10

Of course, from what we have already looked at, the UFOs that are commonly reported look nothing like what Ezekiel reported. There is one aspect of this heavenly chariot, however, that does hold a certain resemblance and might provide more information as to the biological and extradimensional nature of certain UFOs.

The Ophanim

Continuing from where we left off in the previous chapter, Ezekiel reports:

[15] *Now as I beheld the living creatures, behold one wheel upon the earth by the living creatures, with his four faces.*

¹⁶ The appearance of the wheels and their work was like unto the colour of a beryl: and they four had one likeness: and their appearance and their work was as it were a wheel in the middle of a wheel.

¹⁷ When they went, they went upon their four sides: and they turned not when they went.

Ezekiel 1:15-17

The word "wheels" used here was translated from the Hebrew word *"owphan"*, which is where we get the plural *"ophanim"*.[73] By itself, the Hebrew word *"ophanim"* simply means wheels and doesn't denote anything necessarily extraordinary. Many times this word is used for regular, earthly wheels, such as those found on normal, human-made chariots.[74] This word was also used to describe the wheels of the ten bases beneath the lavers in Solomon's temple.[75] However, taken in the context of this passage, Ezekiel is describing something quite different than earthly, man-made wheels; he is describing an actual extradimensional being.

Upon first read of the passage, it would seem these wheels were a part of the living construct that makes up God's chariot. In some ways, this is true. However, they are not connected

---

[73] "Hebrew Lexicon :: H212 (KJV)." Blue Letter Bible. Accessed 22 Dec, 2014. http://www.blueletterbible.org/lang/Lexicon/Lexicon.cfm?Strongs=H212&t=KJV
[74] See Exodus 14:25
[75] See 1 Kings 7:30-33

physically. Verse 15 tells us the wheels were *by* the living creatures; not connected to them. While not connected physically, however, we will see later the wheels were connected in another way.

Giving further description of these wheels, or ophanim, Ezekiel continues:

"As for their rings, they were so high that they were dreadful; and their rings were full of eyes round about them four."

Ezekiel 1:18

The word "rings" comes from the Hebrew word *"gab"* and means *"rim (of a wheel)"*.[76] Ezekiel was describing the rims of these wheels, even saying they were *full of eyes.*

There is an interpretation of this that states the *eyes* were most likely windows of a craft. At first, this may seem plausible. After all, Ezekiel was trying to describe something he had never seen before and would use the best terms he could to describe it. The problem with this, however, is if Ezekiel was trying to describe windows, he could have just as easily used the Hebrew word *"challown"*, which literally means "window".[77] Ezekiel had

---

[76] "Hebrew Lexicon :: H1354 (KJV)." Blue Letter Bible. Accessed 22 Dec, 2014.
http://www.blueletterbible.org/lang/Lexicon/Lexicon.cfm?Strongs=H1354&t=KJV
[77] "Hebrew Lexicon :: H2474 (KJV)." Blue Letter Bible. Accessed 22 Dec, 2014.

access to far simpler and more descriptive Hebrew words he could have used if he was trying to describe something other than what is presented in the text.[78] This is what leads me to believe when Ezekiel writes "eyes", he literally means "eyes" (Figure 19).[79]

Figure 19 - Depiction of the Wheels of Ezekiel's Vision including the Eyes

Next, Ezekiel writes:

[19] *And when the living creatures went, the wheels went by them: and when the living creatures were lifted up from the earth, the wheels were lifted up.*

[20] *Whithersoever the spirit was to go, they went, thither was their spirit to go; and the wheels were lifted up over against them: for the spirit of the living creature was in the wheels.*

[21] *When those went, these went; and when those stood, these stood; and when those were lifted up from the earth, the wheels were lifted up over against them: for the spirit of the living creature was in the wheels.*

Ezekiel 1:19-21

---

http://www.blueletterbible.org/lang/Lexicon/Lexicon.cfm?Strongs=H2474&t=KJV

[78] For more on this, watch Dr. Michael Heiser's presentation of Ezekiel's vision here - http://youtu.be/sflMu19t3QE

[79] The Hebrew word for "eyes" here is *"ayin"*, the same word as we looked at from the book of Zechariah in the previous chapter.

This passage is what tells us the true nature of the ophanim. These were not merely inanimate wheels; they were actually *alive*. We know this because Ezekiel tells us the spirit of the living creatures was in the wheels. The wheels themselves acted as a type of body for the spirits. The wheels were not just an extradimensional mechanical construct. The wheels had life in them.

There are ancient texts that actually refer to the ophanim as a specific class of angel. In the book of Enoch can be found one of these references:

"And He will summon all the host of the heavens, and all the holy ones above, and the host of God, the Cherubic, Seraphin and Ophannin, and all the angels of power, and all the angels of principalities, and the Elect One, and the other powers on the earth (and) over the water On that day shall raise one voice, and bless and glorify and exalt in the spirit of faith, and in the spirit of wisdom, and in the spirit of patience, and in the spirit of mercy, and in the spirit of judgement and of peace, and in the spirit of goodness, and shall all say with one voice: " Blessed is He, and may the name of the Lord of Spirits be blessed for ever and ever. " "[80]

The idea of the ophanim being an actual class of angel is not a new or altogether uncommon idea. The Sephardic Jewish philosopher

---

[80] The book of Enoch 61:10

and astronomer Maimonides wrote that the ophanim are the second class in the hierarchy of angels.[81] Pseudo-Dionysius, in the 4th or 5th century, wrote that the ophanim were among the first sphere of angelic hierarchy.[82]

We can see these wheels in other books of the Bible as well:

"I beheld till the thrones were cast down, and the Ancient of days did sit, whose garment was white as snow, and the hair of his head like the pure wool: his throne was like the fiery flame, and his wheels as burning fire."

Daniel 7:9

One thing is for sure: if the ophanim are indeed a class of angel all their own, then Heaven and its inhabitants are far stranger than we are traditionally led to believe. This is just one of many ways that shows how fascinating the study of extradimensional beings and vehicles can be.

This also brings up some interesting questions concerning the fallen angels mentioned in the Bible. Is it possible different angels from different classes fell? Could there have been a rebellious group of ophanim that fell? Could this explain at least

---

[81] Maimonides *Yad ha-Chazakah: Yesodei ha-Torah*
[82] Pseudo-Dionysius - *De Coelesti Hierarchia* (*On the Celestial Hierarchy*)

some of the modern UFO sightings we see today? Is it possible that certain UFOs might actually be alive?

The Spirits of UFOs

There is one last point we can look at in this chapter. It has been reported that Ben Rich, the director of Lockheed's Skunk Works from 1975 to 1991, admitted that, not only are UFOs real, but that they are powered by a type of ESP.[83] If this is true, perhaps this is an example of man's crude attempt of understanding something spiritual through a scientific lens. Imagine if we saw today what Ezekiel saw in the ancient past. Imagine if we saw the cherubim move wheels without touching them. Would we not assume it was by some form of ESP?

Instead of thinking of it as a power from the mind, perhaps we should be thinking of it as a power from the spirit. After all, Ezekiel stated that the spirits of the cherubim were in the wheels. Wherever the spirit went, the wheels went. Perhaps we are seeing the same sort of thing in some of the modern sightings of UFOs. Perhaps the extradimensional pilot is actually controlling the vehicle by its spirit. Perhaps the spirit itself *is* the pilot and the vehicle is the body. Perhaps, like a fallen version of what Ezekiel

---

[83] http://youtu.be/LX7q--QLz1k

CHAPTER 7

saw, the things we typically recognize as extraterrestrial craft are actually living extradimensional beings.

The Topographical Spacemen

The Nazca Spaceman

One piece of evidence that is sometimes used to support the ancient astronaut theory is that of the Nazca Lines. In southern Peru, north of the town of Nazca, there is an expanse of desert with some very interestingly artistic geoglyphs. The geoglyphs are absolutely enormous and depict many different types of creatures, such as a monkey, a hummingbird, and a spider, that can best be seen from the sky. There is one geoglyph that has received special attention within the ancient astronaut community. This unique geoglyph is known as "The Spaceman" and sometimes "The Giant".[84]

There is a lot of speculation and contention as to the reason for the original crafters of the geoglyphs to include this strange design. The common theory within the ancient astronaut community is that it is depicting a being from another planet that visited long ago. The theory goes on to state that after the alien beings departed Earth, the indigenous people of the area created these geoglyphs in an attempt to call them back. Some will call to attention the presence of Cargo Cults as modern day examples of this type of occurrence.

A Cargo Cult is a type of religion that began when cargo planes during WWII would drop off supplies to the natives of the pacific islands. The islanders, having no real concept of technology, thought these planes and pilots to be agents of the gods. After the war ended and the cargo planes left for good, the islanders would build replicas of the planes out of branches and leaves in an attempt to appease the gods and bring the cargo planes back.[85] Many within the ancient astronaut community believe it is that type of thing we are looking at concerning the Nazca Spaceman. They see it as an attempt by the indigenous people of

[84] http://en.wikipedia.org/wiki/Nazca_Lines
[85] http://www.sjsu.edu/faculty/watkins/cargocult.htm

that area to call back the aliens, who they apparently mistook for gods, after they departed the earth.

The obvious answer to this from certain areas of Christianity is that, if nothing else, this is not depicting an ancient alien but is depicting a regular native of Nazca. Some would even go as far as to suggest it is an ancient fallen angel or Nephilim. Given the odd shape of the head and eyes in the geoglyph, this is a possibility. As we will discover later, either way, the outcome is the same.

Below are two pictures of the same Spaceman geoglyph. The first (Figure 20) is the original and the second (Figure 21) contains a crude overlay to help see the image.

Figure 20 - The Spaceman Geoglyph

Figure 21 - The Spaceman Geoglyph with Overlay

In moving forward, keep one thing in mind the right arm is raised. This may not seem particularly important as of now, especially since the first anomaly we automatically notice is the odd shape of the Spaceman's head and eyes. That does have some importance as well, as we will see, but the main point of importance is the upraised right arm.

The Goat Head of Azazel

What is incredibly interesting is not only the existence of geoglyphs created by man, but also the existence of geoglyphs seemingly created by nature. As we looked at earlier, the book of Enoch describes Mount Hermon as the place where the angels who fell from Heaven touched down on Earth and conspired to mate with the female population. The worst of these angels was named

Azazel, to whom the scapegoat of Leviticus was sent. The fact that the scapegoat is in connection with Azazel is incredibly interesting when we look at the topography of the area.

These are two of the same image of Mount Hermon taken from Google Earth. The first picture (Figure 22) shows the topography of Mount Hermon while the second picture (Figure 23) contains a rough overlay to show the image more clearly.

Figure 22 – Mount Hermon at 33°27'38.21"N and 36°04'29.65"E

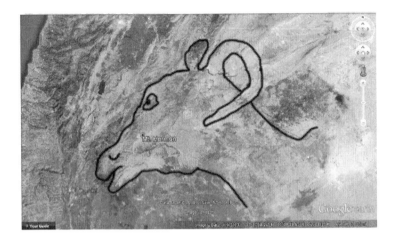

Figure 23 – Mount Hermon with a Goat Head Overlay

This is one example of how a topographical image that is naturally formed can be a shadow of a biblical or extra-biblical account. Keeping this example of Azazel and the goat in mind, there are two other naturally-made topographical images that are strikingly similar to the Nazca Spaceman.

The Mount Hermon Spacemen

The first image we will look at is actually found within the goat head on Mount Hermon. It is more than interesting that this appears in the same location, within the same image, as the goat head referencing Azazel. Here we have the same picture of Mount Hermon we looked at before (Figure 24), only this time with a different rough overlay (Figure 25).

Figure 24 - Mount Hermon

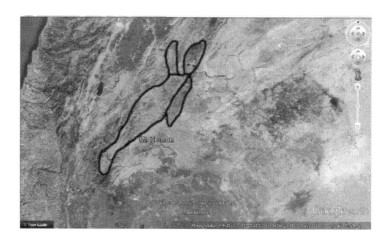

Figure 25 - Mount Hermon with a Spaceman Overlay

The overlay in the bottom picture isn't an exact representation, but it should be enough for you to be able to see the naturally-made geoglyph in the top image. These naturally-made geoglyphs are a bit more difficult to pick out the fine details when presented in a book such as this. To really do this justice, I would highly suggest viewing Mount Hermon directly from Google Earth at the coordinates provided in Figure 22.

The similarities between this naturally-made geoglyph (for ease of reference, we will call it the "Mount Hermon Spaceman") and the man-made Nazca Spaceman of Peru are striking. We see that the right arm is raised up while the left arm is down. What is equally interesting is the difference in head shape. The Nazca Spaceman has a head shape that is more similar to something like the supposed "Star-child" skull.[86] The Mount Hermon Spaceman, however, seems to have an elongated cranium, which is eerily reminiscent of the elongated skulls found in Peru and other places throughout the world.

The fact that the Mount Hermon Spaceman is found in the area where the book of Enoch says the Watchers touched down to mate with human women is profound. It is almost as if this very act burned a shadow into the topography of the mountain to add legitimacy to the event; much like the goat head can point back to Azazel. Now, while the Nazca Spaceman is man-made, it is equally profound that it is found in an area of the world which is known for containing elongated skulls that do not appear to be human. Given the fact that the Mount Hermon Spaceman seems to have an elongated cranium, it would seem to point back to Peru,

---

[86] www.starchildproject.com

where many elongated skulls have been found, and where the Nazca Spaceman can also be found. There is still one more naturally-made geoglyph and one more connection that can be made.

In the past, much study has been done on the connection between Mount Hermon and Roswell, NM. Author and researcher David Flynn was the first to discover that Mount Hermon (using the old Paris Prime Meridian) is located at 33.33 degrees latitude and 33.33 degrees longitude. The number 33 has very strong occult significance. What is especially interesting is the site of the supposed UFO crash near Roswell, NM in 1947 is also on the 33.33 degree latitude line. Surprisingly, if you multiply the latitude of the crash site by the constant of Pi (33.33 X 3.14), you come to 104.6, which just so happens to be the longitude of the same crash site.[87] The research done by David Flynn in this area has been absolutely fascinating to me since the time I first heard it. It was building off that research that led to my interest in searching for the Topographical Spacemen after a chance noticing of the Mount Hermon Spaceman.

Once I saw the topographical image of the Mount Hermon Spaceman for myself, it reminded me of the Nazca Spaceman. I noticed the connection between the elongated skulls that have been discovered in Peru and the elongated cranium of the Mount

---

[87] http://watchervault.com/tag/mt-hermon/

Hermon Spaceman. For me, however, this was not enough. If I am going to put any stock into something such as this, I need to be able to confirm it for myself to know if there really is something there. I decided that if this was true, if there was any legitimacy to this connection and given the fact of the connection between Mount Hermon and Roswell, NM, there should be a naturally-made spaceman-type image in the topography of Roswell. Just any trick of light and shadow upon the contours of the land would not be enough. If this was to be true, it would have to share the same basic resemblance of the first two. The right hand should be raised and the left arm should be down. Also, the head should have an unusual shape. I knew if I found something that had anything less than these qualities; it would be a waste of time and would not be included in this chapter. Being a biblical researcher, especially in the field of eschatology, I was prepared for this outcome as it has happened many times before. Having low expectations for finding anything at all, I searched Google Earth. What I discovered was quite surprising.

The Roswell Spaceman

Just as the last set of images, these next pictures can be difficult to see in a book such as this (Figures 26 and 27). I have included another rough overlay, just as in the previous images. However, to really do these images justice, I would again suggest using Google Earth to view them yourself at the provided coordinates.

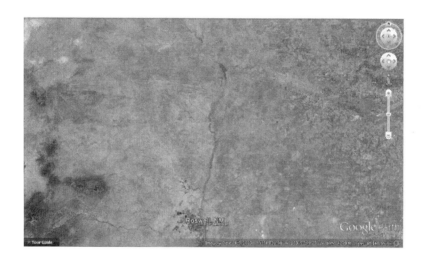

Figure 26 - Roswell, NM at 33°49'21.98"N and 103°57'49.23"W

Figure 27 - Roswell, NM with Overlay

I immediately noticed the details I was looking for. I saw the upraised right arm. I saw the left arm was down at the side. I even saw that the shape of the head was irregular.

The shape of the Roswell Spaceman's head is unique, just as the other two were. In fact, the head shape of this one is extremely similar to the descriptions of the alien beings that were claimed to be recovered at the Roswell UFO crash site. I noticed that this easily resembled a race of supposed aliens called the "Greys".

I was both surprised and excited to find this, especially with it being a bit north of Roswell, which is closer to where the original crash site was reported as having occurred. However, I still like to play these things as safely as possible. There was one other conclusion that I had to test as a possibility before I would be comfortable posting these findings. I had to make sure that I wasn't just seeing Topographical Spacemen everywhere.

I picked a few different sites where I would expect to find the same thing. This was to test my eyes and my own reasoning. I figured the next best place to look would be Phoenix, Arizona due to the popular Phoenix Lights sightings. After long searching of the topography on and around Phoenix, AZ, I found nothing. Next, I tried Stephenville, TX because of the mass sightings there. Again, I found nothing. I tried a few other random areas on Earth and even tried checking the topography of the Moon and Mars.

Once again, I found nothing, nothing, and more nothing. By this time I was convinced that it was not just my eyes playing tricks on me or just my imagination creating the Topographical Spacemen. I knew there was something more to it. It was then that I made the discovery that tied everything together to make some sort of sense out of these strange images. It was then that I discovered the Orion connection, which is something we will look at in the next chapter.

Mount Hermon and Roswell Reconnected

As we touched on before, there seems to be a strong connection between Mount Hermon and Roswell, NM. There are mathematical/geographical connections as well as the connection between the naturally-made Topographical Spacemen. What is even more interesting is there seems to be a type of red zone in the two areas.

Mount Hermon was the place where the original 200 watchers touched down on Earth to mate with human women, according to the book of Enoch. The Mount Hermon Spaceman is found at that location and seems to be connected to the Orion constellation, which in itself points back to Nimrod. We know from the book of Genesis that Nimrod was the first shadow of the end-time Antichrist. Nimrod led the world in the construction of the Tower of Babel in an attempt to reach into Heaven in rebellion to God. Due to these circumstances, there seems to be a strong connection between Mount Hermon and the Tower of Babel.

As we looked at earlier, we can think of Mount Hermon as the center of all the original collective activity, deception, and rebellion to God. We can also look at the Tower of Babel as the edge of where this rebellion ended up before God stepped in and judged the people of the earth. This gives us the center and the edge of, what I will call, the Middle East Red Zone.

Within this red zone, we can find many biblical locations that tie back to rebellion against God. The location where Pharaoh kept the enslaved children of Israel is found within this red zone. Babylon is within this area, which ties back to the woman in the ephah in chapter five of the book of Zechariah. The whole nation of Israel, in fact, is found within this red zone, as well as the surrounding nations. We can tie that back to the surrounding Nephilim tribes back in the days of Joshua.

The interesting thing is the location where the Bible says Noah's ark settled in Mount Ararat is outside of this red zone. It is as if God took Noah out of this area to protect him and his children. Later, however, Noah's family lineage ended up rebelling against God in the days of Nimrod, right on the edge of the Middle East Red Zone.

Here is a map (Figure 28) from Google Maps showing this red zone with Mount Hermon at its center and the location of the Tower of Babel at its edge.

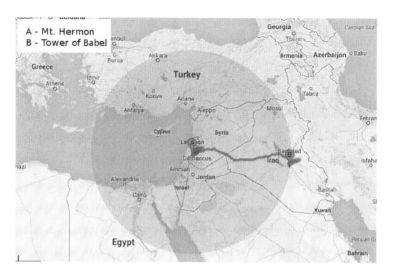

Figure 28 - The Middle East Red Zone

Next is a map (Figure 29), also from Google Maps, showing the America Red Zone in the same relative geographical size and area of the Middle East Red Zone, only with Roswell, NM as its center instead of Mount Hermon.

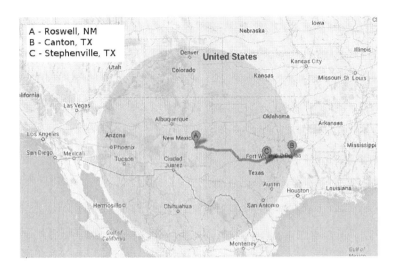

Figure 29 - The American Red Zone

If the connection between Mount Hermon and Roswell, NM is true, we should expect to be able to see this same type of red zone around Roswell. If the appearance of extradimensional beings and vehicles connect to Mount Hermon in antiquity, and if there is an America Red Zone that is the same size and relative location as the Middle East Red Zone, it should contain some of the biggest and most well-known UFO sightings and encounters known.

Within the America Red Zone, we actually do find the locations of some of the most compelling UFO encounters and sightings to date. The relative location to the Tower of Babel, to the best of my own estimation, seems to be located right around

Canton, Texas, which has seen its fair share of UFOs and unexplained anomalies. Just west of Canton, TX is Stephenville, TX, which is the location of the well-known Stephenville Lights sightings. Also within the America Red Zone is Phoenix, Arizona, which is the location of the Phoenix Lights sightings. We also find Denver, Colorado, the home to the Denver Airport, which has many different sinister stories and claims attached to it involving all sorts of conspiracies and evil intent. The Zone of Silence in Mexico, a place where radio signals fail and reports of alien encounters are numerous, is within this red zone. We also find the claimed location of the original discovery of the Star-child skull found within this area as well.[88] Of course, there are other mysterious connections. When fully delving into it, the strange locations seem endless. I have only provided a short list.

At the absolute core of this mystery, I believe we are looking at a shadow between Mount Hermon and Roswell, NM. I believe we can look at everything that happened in antiquity surrounding Mount Hermon as a shadow of what happened, what is happening, and what will happen in and around the area of Roswell. When considering all of these strange sightings and encounters we are dealing with in our day, I believe we can look back to the time of the 200 watchers to understand what is happening. In ancient times, the fallen angels presented

---

[88] http://en.wikipedia.org/wiki/Starchild_skull

themselves as gods. Today, they are presenting themselves as a superior race of alien beings from another planet. It is the same deception they have always promulgated. The only difference is the packaging.

Interstellar Prophecies

The Orion Connection

Building off from the last chapter, after I had discovered the Roswell Spaceman and tested my conclusions against topographies of other areas, I began to seriously contemplate what the connection between these three images could be. There was something about the upraised right arm in each image that really jumped out at me. I noticed a similarity with the Orion constellation. The constellation of Orion has an upraised right arm, just as the Topographical Spacemen.

There is an interesting theory that makes the connection between Orion and the Biblical figure Nimrod. The basic theory is that after Nimrod tried to set up his one-world religion and government (something I also address in my book *Disclosure*) and after God scattered the nations and confused their languages, the people of the earth would still tell the same stories of what happened. These stories would be all in different languages, of course, so a person like Nimrod would be referred to by many different names. According to this theory, one of the many names attributed to Nimrod was Orion.

The interesting thing about the Orion constellation is it is depicted as fighting against a lion. Orion has an upraised club in his right hand, and in his left hand, is holding back a lion. The lion could represent Jesus Christ, as He is the lion of the tribe of Judah. There is also a possible connection between Orion/Nimrod and the Beast of Revelation that comes up out of the bottomless pit. This makes sense concerning our Topographical Spacemen, especially the naturally-made two, and our idea of the fulfillment of end-time prophecy. There was still one feature of the Nazca Spaceman specifically, however, that was bothering me in relating them to Orion. It was that of the vertical line.

The Omega Star

I knew that the vertical line in the images would have to be addressed if there was any real connection between Orion and the Nazca Spaceman. It wasn't until I researched the constellation of Orion for myself that I learned the astounding significance. It is not depicted in any picture or map of the Orion constellation that I have found but, to my surprise, there is a line of stars that bisects Orion.

Here are two pictures of the Orion constellation. These pictures are clear illustrations that show the stars that make up the vertical line from Orion's legs to his neck. The first picture (Figure 30) is untouched and the second (Figure 31) contains white lines to connect the appropriate stars.

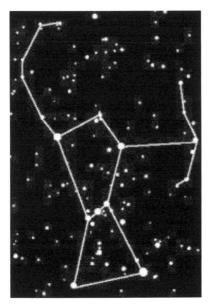

Figure 30 - The Orion Constellation

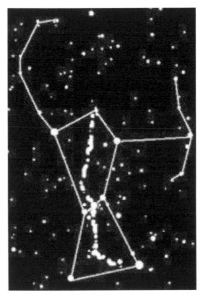

*Figure 31 - The Orion Constellation
with Overlay*

Here is a picture of the Orion constellation (Figure 32) that contains the names of the stars that create the outline of the constellation as well as those that are found within.

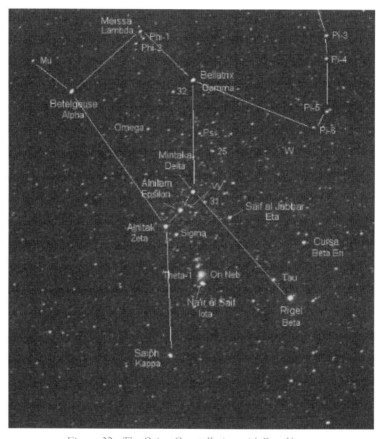

Figure 32 - The Orion Constellation with Star Names

We can see that there is a line of stars that seem to split the image in half. The most noticeable star in this vertical line is found right in the middle of Orion's torso. It is named Omega (sometimes called Omega Orionis or Omega Ori).[89] We can see the vertical line go up from Orion's legs to his neck.

This is the same thing we see in the Nazca Spaceman that we looked at earlier. It leads one to wonder why the indigenous people created it that way. What is even more interesting than that, however, is the naturally-made Mount Hermon Spaceman and Roswell Spaceman have their right arms raised, just like Orion.

Speculative Interpretations

The reasons I have to explain the common features found in these images are speculative at best. In all my research, I could not find a clear-cut and easily defined reason for these similarities. I do not have all the answers and I have not connected all of the dots (no pun intended). However, I do not mind providing my best guess for what is being signified. Please keep in mind, as it bears repeating, this is nothing more than a guess.

I do believe, as I explained in *Disclosure*, that it is possible Nimrod did something to himself to become of the Nephilim. I believe this may have had something to do with genetic manipulation or some sort of occult practice. The details on how it happened are not clear, but the Bible does seem to indicate that

---

[89] http://stars.astro.illinois.edu/sow/omegaori.html

something happened in order for Nimrod to go from fully human to part human, part Nephilim (or part fallen angel, false god, etc.).

I also believe that, due to the scattering of languages, Nimrod and Orion might be essentially the same person in antiquity. This would mean Orion would have been part human and part god.[90] I believe it is possible that the vertical line in the constellation of Orion is signifying this fact.

There is a theory that states Nimrod/Orion is the coming Antichrist or was at least oppressed by the same antichrist spirit that will embody the future Antichrist. If it is true that Nimrod/Orion was a shadow of the future Antichrist, then it is possible the Antichrist could also be part human and part god. The Antichrist may start off as human but, through advances in technology or occult practices, may accept a splice of genetic material from the serpent himself, thereby making the Antichrist part human and part god. This splice of genetic material could also be offered to the world from the Antichrist and could be what we recognize as the mark of the Beast. The human population would accept the mark and, in like manner, become part human and part god.

The Topographical Spacemen could be a shadow, warning, or even prophecy of that event. They each are enormous

---

[90] The lowercase "g" in "god" is signifying these are demons or fallen angels.

and facing the sky, possibly meant for the constellation Orion. They each have their right hand raised, which seems to be a sign of loyalty. Not only does it mimic the Orion constellation, but it also ties back to the mark of the Beast being accepted in the forehead or the right hand. This could be a way of alluding to that future loyalty to the Antichrist, especially given the clear connections between the future Antichrist and Nimrod/Orion.

Orion has the club and is using it against the lion. The Topographical Spacemen are different. They do not have weapons and are not depicted as fighting. It is almost as if to say they are leaving the supernatural fighting aspect to their master and are supporting him from the sidelines in total loyalty. Just as the serpent gives his power to the Antichrist in the book of Revelation, it seems these beings are doing the same.

The right arm being raised and the fact that they have abnormal head shapes may show that these are not merely human beings. These are some sort of cross between the supernatural and the natural. The raised right arm, mimicking Orion, could be a direct reference to accepting the mark of the Beast and worshiping him. The unusual head shapes may show what we have been seeing concerning the Grays, elongated craniums, and encounters with extradimensional beings.

The elongated skull could tie back to ancient, nonhuman skulls that have been found, especially in Peru. The head shape of the Nazca Spaceman seems to be reminiscent of the Star-child skull and could be depicting another type of hybrid between angel and man. The head shape of the Roswell Spaceman seems identical to the supposed alien Grays that people have been reporting and seeing. There are people in the world who would say these are depicting extraterrestrial beings. However, in my humble opinion these are not beings from another world we are dealing with. I believe we are seeing depictions, both manufactured and natural, of fallen angel/human hybrids.

The Topographical Spacemen could be a reference to the days of Noah, which Jesus warned prophetically warned against. These geoglyphs seem to be depicting ancient beings. These ancient beings could be a shadow of what is to come. I believe it is possible we could be seeing a return of these beings in some form of the flesh in our future.

The Nazi Salute

When we think back to images of Hitler and the Nazi salute, we see some interesting

Figure 33 - Hitler giving the Nazi Salute

similarities to the topographical spacemen (Figure 33). This is certainly a speculative connection, but given the theology Hitler adhered to concerning the occult and UFOs, there might be something here.[91] Notice the raised right arm. We could even call attention to the coat that provides a bisected line, such as with Orion and the Nazca Spaceman. Wikipedia has this to say about the Nazi salute:

The Nazi salute or Hitler salute (German: Hitlergruß – literally Hitler Greeting) is a gesture that was used as a greeting in Nazi Germany. The salute is performed by extending the right arm in the air with a straightened hand. Usually, the person offering the salute would say "Heil Hitler!" (Hail Hitler!), "Heil, mein Führer!" (Hail, my leader!), or "Sieg heil!" (Hail victory!). It was adopted in the 1930s by the Nazi Party to signal obedience to the party's leader – Adolf Hitler – and to glorify the German nation (and later the German war effort).[92]

There have been connections made, by other researchers as well as myself, to show Hitler could have been a shadow of the coming Antichrist.[93]

I could even see a possibility of there being a connection between the Antichrist and Azazel. At the very least, shadows do seem to exist. The book of Enoch says that sin was ascribed to

---

[91] For more information on this, check out *Power Quest* books 1 and 2 by S. Douglas Woodward – www.faith-happens.com

[92] http://en.wikipedia.org/wiki/Nazi_salute

[93] I deal with this in *Disclosure* as well as my blog post *Haman to Hitler: The Secret Nazi Prophecy*, which can be found at http://joshpeckdisclosure.blogspot.com/2014/08/haman-to-hitler-secret-nazi-prophecy.html

Azazel. The coming Antichrist is referred to as the man of sin in 2 Thessalonians 2:3. We also know from the book of Revelation that the Beast comes up out of the bottomless pit. This seems to be the place that Azazel is imprisoned in the book of Enoch.

As it stands right now, I do not know if we can use what we know about Hitler and Azazel to identify the coming Antichrist. I would not go as far as to say that Azazel is the coming Antichrist or is even the spirit of antichrist itself, but I do see similarities. At the very least, I do believe we can look at attributes and examples from the account of Azazel as a shadow pointing toward the coming Antichrist.

That is about the best I can speculate concerning the meaning of these cryptic images. I do believe it is a shadow that should point us directly back to the pages of the Bible to discover the reality of the situation. There could come a time in our very near future when we will have to deal with these things personally.

The Duality of Interpreting the Stars

As we have seen with the Orion constellation, there are things laid out for us in the stars that may reveal the intentions of a very ancient and malevolent adversary. We can look at each constellation in the heavens from the perspective of the enemy to see what evils are coming our way. However, we can view them from another perspective and find a great message of hope.

The first chapter of the book of Genesis gives the account of the creation of stars:

"And God said, Let there be lights in the firmament of the heaven to divide the day from the night; and let them be for signs, and for seasons, and for days, and years:"

Genesis 1:14

This tells us these lights were created for two main purposes: for timekeeping and for signs. All throughout the Bible, God has used the stars to convey messages to His people and the world. The best example of this is the announcement of the birth of Jesus to the wise men:

9 When they had heard the king, they departed; and, lo, the star, which they saw in the east, went before them, till it came and stood over where the young child was.

10 When they saw the star, they rejoiced with exceeding great joy.

11 And when they were come into the house, they saw the young child with Mary his mother, and fell down, and worshipped him: and when they had opened their treasures, they presented unto him gifts; gold, and frankincense and myrrh.

Matthew 2:9-11

168

What is interesting is the idea that the whole plan of God, the entire gospel from a biblical perspective, can be found in the stars. This idea was made popular by E.W. Bullinger and Joseph A. Seiss in the 1800s. Below is listed out the twelve signs of the Zodiac with the common biblical interpretations:

1. Virgo (the Virgin) – Sometimes portrayed as Eve but most often as the virgin Mary.

2. Libra (the Scales) – Showing the balance of creation that was lost after the fall resulting in a need for sin to be accountable.

3. Scorpio (the Scorpion) – Sin brings death.

4. Sagittarius (the Archer) – The fiery darts of the enemy, showing the influence of fallen angels on humanity.

5. Capricorn (the Goat-fish) – Corruption of God's creation; specifically biological life. Sometimes the goat is associated with Azazel and the fish with Leviathan.

6. Aquarius (the Water-bearer) – Judgment in the form of the flood in the days of Noah.

7. Pisces (the Fish) – God's remnant from those who survived the flood.

8. Aries (the Ram) – The need for sacrifice to atone for sin.

9. Taurus (the Bull) – Resurrection

10. Gemini (the Twins) – The dual nature of Jesus Christ: God and man.

11. Cancer (the Crab) – The gathering of the redeemed.

12. Leo (the Lion) – Jesus the King.

There are certain additions and variations to this list depending on who is presenting the information. Author James Kennedy associates the balances of Daniel 5:27 in his interpretation of Libra.[94] He also associates Psalm 21:12, concerning the drawn bow, and Psalm 45:5, concerning the sharp arrows, with Sagittarius.[95] Marilyn Hickey includes the goat of the sin offering of Leviticus 10:16 for Capricorn.[96] She also equates the wild ox of Psalm 92:10 with Taurus.[97] Kenneth Fleming includes the Lion of the tribe of Judah of Revelation 5:5 in his interpretation of the sign Leo.[98] Kennedy gives the interpretation of the twins of Gemini as "Judge and Ruler".[99] Fleming describes them as "Prince and Savior".[100] For Virgo, Kennedy includes interpretations of the virgin Mary, the desired Son, the despised sin offering, and "the coming One".[101] Fleming adds "the coming Shepherd".[102]

---

[94] D. James Kennedy, *The Real Meaning of the Zodiac* (Ft. Lauderdale: CRM, 1989), 29–36.

[95] Ibid., 49–58.

[96] Marilyn Hickey, *Signs in the Heavens* (Denver: Marilyn Hickey Ministries, 1984), 51–59.

[97] Ibid., 89–100.

[98] Kenneth C. Fleming, *God's Voice in the Stars* (Neptune, NJ: Loizeaux Brothers, 1988), 135–141.

[99] Kennedy, 107–115.

[100] Fleming, 115–121.

[101] Kennedy, 19–25.

[102] Fleming, 35–41.

Joseph A. Seiss identifies Scorpio as the battle between the serpent (Satan) and Jesus Christ.[103]

Clearly there are a lot of things that can be looked at in a study such as this. There are even those who would say every star of every constellation in the heavens proclaims the gospel of Jesus Christ in some way. Conversely, there are those who would say, from an astrological and unbiblical perspective, the stars proclaim everything we could ever want to know about ourselves and our future. Thus is the duality: we can either look to the heavens and try to go at it alone or we can allow the one who created them in the first place to guide us.[104]

Interview with S. Douglas Woodward

 S. Douglas Woodward is author of the book *Blood Moon: Biblical Signs of the Coming Apocalypse,* which expertly deals in topics relating to signs in the heavens. He is also the author of many other books dealing with the study of Bible prophecy. I have interviewed Doug

---

[103] Joseph A. Seiss, *The Gospel in the Stars* (Grand Rapids: Kregal, 1978), 43-51.
[104] For more information on the Zodiac from a biblical and historical perspective, check out *The Pre-flood Origins of Astrology* by Dr. Ken Johnson.

numerous times on my show *The Sharpening* and could think of no one better to provide his perspective in this area. A special thanks goes out to Doug for taking the time to provide his expertise in this interview.

*   *   *

JOSH PECK: What is the meaning of the word "signs" in Genesis 1:14?

DOUG WOODWARD: The Hebrew word is transliterated '*owth*' and pronounced 'oath'. The term has many uses in the Old Testament. *Signs* is often connected with the word '*mopheth*' (aka 'wonders' pronounced 'mo faith')… as in the phrase "signs and wonders". (Deuteronomy 6:22, Neh. 9:10, Jeremiah 32:20) There is almost a play on words here when one considers the English pronunciation of these Hebrew words… True signs and wonders are like "oaths that give us mo' faith." That is why the most important aspect of 'signs' is the covenant aspect. A sign is established by God as a means to declare a covenant. The same term is used for the 'rainbow' (*Noahic Covenant*) and for 'circumcision' (*Abrahamic Covenant*). A sign implies a commitment or a promise. It is not just intended to 'wow' someone, although 'shock and awe' certainly happens and appear referenced in respect to the signs shown to the nemesis of Moses, Egypt's Pharaoh, and to Nebuchadnezzar, King of Babylon, the patron of Daniel. We must remember that Jesus said, "A wicked and adulterous generation seeketh after a sign," (Matthew 16:4) While signs are a means of shock and awe, they also imply judgment or impending judgment to those who oppose God. When Moses reminds the Hebrews of the mighty works of God that He did to save them from the armies of Pharaoh, he does so with an element of "fear and trembling." God judged Pharaoh. If we don't walk in His righteousness, He will judge us too.

JOSH PECK: How is looking to heavenly signs from a biblical aspect different than astrology?

DOUG WOODWARD: Astrology is a means to predict the future, believing that there are gods associated with the stars and these gods affect the lives of humans. One wonders about the link between stars and angels and whether in ancient times there was an assumed link between fallen angels connected to certain stars and the influence they have on us. We think of the passage in Job which describes the angels as stars: "The morning stars sang together" (Job 38:7) when the Lord created the heavens and the earth. It is interesting also that biblical signs in the heavens tend to also be tied to prophetic matters. The rainbow in the heavens promised (and predicted) that no flood would ever again destroy all life on earth. The star of Bethlehem affirmed the birth of the

Messiah... and tradition suggests that the same star heralded the birth of Moses (there are many parallels between Moses and Christ—however, that is another study). Essentially, though, heavenly signs are meant to demonstrate the providence of God, his power and control over all that happens. There appears to be a synchronization of salvation events on the earth with the timing of events in the heavens—the position of planets, the moon, the sun, eclipses, and so on. We will talk about this a bit more in responding to the next question.

JOSH PECK: What are some examples of prophetic signs in the heavens and how were they fulfilled?

DOUG WOODWARD: The most frequent example would be in relation to the calendar, specifically the new moon and the full moon, and the correlation to the Hebrew high holy days. To a great extent, these events were directly intended to tie to lunar events because the Hebrew Calendar is a lunar (vs. solar) calendar. If we think in terms of the Passover signaling the protection provided by the lamb's blood on the doorpost of the Hebrews in Egypt, and its foreshadowing fulfilled in crucifixion of the Lamb of God (Jesus Christ), we can see how a heavenly sign was connected to earthly events. It becomes more dramatic when we consider the exodus event of the Hebrews passing through the Red Sea three days after leaving Egypt (foreshadowing the resurrection of Jesus three days after his death), the key salvation events on earth were reflected by the timing of the full moon on earth coinciding with these key events.

Going deeper, if we believe that the star of Bethlehem was a conjunction of planets signaling the birth of the Messiah, it would be no surprise that the 'three kings of orient are' who studied the stars and their movements would come looking for the Messiah when the stars were aligned according to an oral tradition that existed predicting a star would appear signaling Messiah's birth (these 'wise men' from the East, were most likely the Magi founded by Daniel the prophet roughly 530 years before Christ was born). If we assume these matters are historical fact, then each of the heavenly bodies were symbolically significant. To be more specific, it appears that the conjunction of planets (known as 'wandering stars' due to their retrograde movements when they appear to move backwards) may have comprised the Bethlehem star. One such conjunction appears likely to be a good candidate for this sign of the birth of Messiah. It involved Jupiter (which was traditionally associated with kingship) with Venus (traditionally associated with a virgin) appearing in the constellation of Leo (also associated with kingship) in the year 2 BC. More recent research suggests that King Herod died in 1 BC (not 4 AD as others have proposed during the past fifty years or so. If so, the timing of the conjunction before his death is necessary to align with the details of the biblical account.[105]

JOSH PECK: Can we use signs in the heavens to determine what things might occur in the future?

DOUG WOODWARD: If we are trying to find out very specific things, I think we are treading in dangerous waters and may be doing the work of astrology. However, if we are looking only at the broad brush strokes of the stars in the heavens and their connections to the Bible's story of God's work to save humankind, our search might be fruitful. Indeed, we might be surprised to learn that the gospel is written in the stars, according to the old work by E. W. Bullinger (1837-1913) (see his book, *The Witness in the Stars*). Bullinger affirms that the constellations tell the story of the Bible, from Genesis to Revelation. For instance, we can point to the vision in Revelation 12:1-4 in which the dragon stands ready to pounce on the offspring of the virgin, an account which is a small subset of the gospel in the stars. We read:

[1] And there appeared a great wonder in heaven; a woman clothed with the sun, and the moon under her feet, and upon her head a crown of twelve stars:

---

[105] See http://www.astronomynotes.com/history/bethlehem-star.html for an intelligent discussion on the topic.

² And she being with child cried, travailing in birth, and pained to be delivered.

³ And there appeared another wonder in heaven; and behold a great red dragon, having seven heads and ten horns, and seven crowns upon his heads.

⁴ And his tail drew the third part of the stars of heaven, and did cast them to the earth: and the dragon stood before the woman which was ready to be delivered, for to devour her child as soon as it was born.

We see all kinds of connections between the stars and signs in the heavens and the story of Jesus' birth, a birth of Messiah nearly thwarted by the Dragon's use of Herod's rage, slaying all the boys 2 and under in the region in and surrounding Judah. The third part of the stars of heaven being pulled away from God and cast to the earth (again another reference to the connection between angels and stars) is also asserted here. The exact meaning and especially the timing of this event is subject to great debate in theology, both in the past and today.

But, are we able to predict events based upon signs in the heavens? In our day, of course, the teachings of Tacoma pastor Mark Biltz and San Antonio pastor John Hagee, assert "Yes, very definitely." They have popularized the viewpoint that we are on the cusp of the Second Coming and these 'tetrads' (four blood moons over a two-year period occurring exactly on these Jewish holidays) are sure signs of that fact. In other words, according to these teachers, the current blood moons occurring on Passover and Sukkoth in 2014 and 2015 coincide… foretelling the imminent return of Jesus. Indeed, Biltz has predicted that the final blood moon in September of 2015 will kick off the final seven years known as Daniel's 70th Week. Of course, this is a long story in itself with the debate joined by others such as Mark Hitchcock of Edmond, Oklahoma, and many others who think such 'date setting' is wild speculation doing more harm than good.

I have taken a middle ground in this debate in my book *Blood Moon: Biblical Signs of the Coming Apocalypse*, pointing out what we are discussing here, that heavenly signs can reinforce God's providence, but they remain ambiguous. The specific darkening of the sun and moon, the turning of the moon to blood, etc., seem to coincide with specific events sometime during the final week of Daniel and not before as Biltz and Hagee teach. Specifically they signal the Day of the Lord, which I believe is not synonymous with Daniel's 70th Week, but is likely directly connected (perhaps synonymous) with the so-called Great Tribulation, which most scholars teach comprises the final 3.5 lunar years or the second half of Daniel's 70th Week.

Note what the scripture (Revelation 6:12-14) teaches will happen when these important telltale signs appear:

CHAPTER 9

12 And I beheld when he had opened the sixth seal, and, lo, there was a great earthquake; and the sun became black as sackcloth of hair, and the moon became as blood;

13 And the stars of heaven fell unto the earth, even as a fig tree casteth her untimely figs, when she is shaken of a mighty wind.

14 And the heaven departed as a scroll when it is rolled together; and every mountain and island were moved out of their places.

When the moon turns to blood and the sun is darkened, we see other more dramatic signs. We see the stars falling from heaven (perhaps another symbolic representation of Satan and his angels being cast out of heaven and falling to earth—another reference to the vision of Revelation 12), the heavens departing like a scroll rolled together, and finally every mountain and island moved out of their places. These images (which I believe will have a literal fulfillment), could be achieved by a change in the location of earth's magnetic poles or even a complete rotational reversal. We don't know how these things will occur or what causes them to happen. However, we can suppose that such changes would not be subtle. Regarding this Sixth Seal, many suggest, and I agree, that with the Sixth Seal, we are seeing transpire the actual resurrection and rapture of 1 Corinthians 15, which has physical consequences on the earth. The argument that it is in this sequence within Revelation at which point the resurrection of believers and the rapture occurs is the position taken in the new book by Jacob

Prasch, *Harpazo: The IntraSeal Rapture of the Church*. This is also argued by others such as my friend David W. Lowe. Additionally, I was privileged to write a foreword to the book written by David, *Then His Voice Shook the Earth* (see Hebrews 12:26 for the phrase referenced in David's title), which provides a compelling argument that *with resurrections come earthquakes*, and the collective impact of perhaps a billion resurrections and hundreds of millions of individuals being raptured all at the same 'twinkling of an eye' could send the earth reeling—literally—backwards.

JOSH PECK: Why is it important to consider the heavens in terms of prophecy?

DOUG WOODWARD: Certainly, we have discussed in the previous question the various connections between signs in the heavens and prophetic events on earth. I stop short of saying we can predict with certainty when events happen by studying the signs in the heavens, the movements of the planets and the stars, the timing of blood moons, solar eclipses, etc. There is so much symbolic language interwoven into the visions involving the heavenly signs in Revelation, if we want to assert their literal fulfillment (how these things will come to pass), it still requires significant speculation. However, I find the signs in the heavens important and their main point indispensable: these signs testify to the providence of God and the fact that our Creator is a God of details, who holds the whole world in His hands and, for that matter, all of the universe. That is pretty crucial to the worldview of the Bible.

JOSH PECK: What do you see taking place in our near future?

DOUG WOODWARD: This question could generate a book in itself. However, a short answer is that many are asserting that we are in *the last of the last days*. I believe that is true. I believe that signs in the heavens and on the earth testify that God is a great 'geometer' too. My frequent co-author, Douglas W Krieger, has written about this in great detail in his book, for which once again I was privileged to write a foreword, *Signs in the Heavens and On the Earth*. I strongly suggest reading his book to probe more deeply into the matter of how the creation itself testifies to the glory and providence of God, and may give us definite clues of the timing of Christ's Second Coming.

So, for further study, I recommend Doug Krieger's work on signs. He has done more research on these topics than anyone with whom I am familiar. David Lowe's book is very well done and provides insights into the Book of Revelation and the meaning of 'the last trumpet,' the meaning of tribulation and Great Tribulation, the sequence of the seals in the chronology of the last days, and a number of other things. I remain a strong advocate for David's work today—it is vastly underrated and that is a shame. I think my book, *Blood Moon*, is a much more biblical take on the Blood Moon phenomenon and so I recommend it too.

*   *   *

Make sure to check out *Blood Moon: Biblical Signs of the Coming Apocalypse* and other titles by S. Douglas Woodward.[106] Visit www.Faith-Happens.com for more information on Doug, his work, and his ministry.

---

[106] *Blood Moon* is available at http://www.amazon.com/Blood-Moon-Biblical-Coming-Apocalypse/dp/1495239578

The Dwelling of God

The Temple and the Spirit

In the beginning of this book, we looked at the Old Testament to get an idea of what the earthly temple of God looked like. Later on, we saw how God has a type of chariot for His throne. We discovered God's chariot is made of living beings: the cherubim. This could lead us to wonder, is there anything else God has that is literally created from living beings? If His chariot is made of cherubim, of what is His eternal dwelling made?

There is a truly beautiful concept taught in the Bible that answers these questions. It is a concept that is unique among all other theologies in the world. We can begin in our understanding with the words of Paul to the Corinthians:

"Know ye not that ye are the temple of God, and that the Spirit of God dwelleth in you?"

1 Corinthians 3:16

There are two ideas as to what this passage is referring. The first idea states that this is meant to be understood as referencing the entire body of believers; the body of Christ as a whole is the temple and the Spirit of God dwells in that body. The second idea states this is referring to the individual Christian; each one of us acts as a temple of God and He dwells in everyone individually. Personally, I believe both ideas are accurate. I believe God dwells in the Church *and* in the individual Christian. One support for this view is the account if the indwelling of the Holy Spirit.

[1] And when the day of Pentecost was fully come, they were all with one accord in one place.

[2] And suddenly there came a sound from heaven as of a rushing mighty wind, and it filled all the house where they were sitting.

[3] And there appeared unto them cloven tongues like as of fire, and it sat upon each of them.

CHAPTER 10

⁴ And they were all filled with the Holy Ghost, and began to speak with other tongues, as the Spirit gave them utterance.

Acts 2:1-4

We can find examples supporting both ideas in this passage. Notice in verse 1 it says they were all in one place and with one accord. The individuals were gathered together with one common mindset. This shows how the group was made up of individuals, yet was acting as a single entity. In verse 3 it states that cloven tongues appeared and *sat upon each of them*. This demonstrates that they each had an individual experience. Verse 4, by the singular language used, shows us that the source of this was one Spirit: the Spirit of God. This passage can be used to show that the Holy Spirit dwells in each believer individually *and* as a whole.

For the purpose of this chapter, I mainly want to focus on the individual aspect. Each and every one of us who has invited Him to do so has the Spirit of God dwelling in us. We are even told exactly where He dwells in the first verse we looked at. If we can view ourselves as the temple of God, we can compare that with the temple in the Old Testament. The temple was made of three parts: the outer court, the inner court, and the Holy of Holies. The Holy of Holies was the innermost part of the temple where God would dwell. We too are made of three parts: the body, soul, and spirit. If we are God's temple, our spirit would be comparable to the Holy of Holies. By contrast, our physical bodies would be comparable to the outer court. Paul talked about the body and the spirit in his writing to the Romans.

18 For I know that in me (that is, in my flesh,) dwelleth no good thing: for to will is present with me; but how to perform that which is good I find not.

19 For the good that I would I do not: but the evil which I would not, that I do.

20 Now if I do that I would not, it is no more I that do it, but sin that dwelleth in me.

Romans 7:18-20

Later in Romans:

9 But ye are not in the flesh, but in the Spirit, if so be that the Spirit of God dwell in you. Now if any man have not the Spirit of Christ, he is none of his.

10 And if Christ be in you, the body is dead because of sin; but the Spirit is life because of righteousness.

11 But if the Spirit of him that raised up Jesus from the dead dwell in you, he that raised up Christ from the dead shall also quicken your mortal bodies by his Spirit that dwelleth in you.

Romans 8:9-11

This can be used to show that the physical body is subject to sin, death, and decay, yet the Spirit of God, dwelling in our spirit, triumphs over all of that. There is another interesting and truly encouraging thing we can consider.

¹⁵ For we have not an high priest which cannot be touched with the feeling of our infirmities; but was in all points tempted like as we are, yet without sin.

¹⁶ Let us therefore come boldly unto the throne of grace, that we may obtain mercy, and find grace to help in time of need.

Hebrews 4:15-16

This passage is telling us how God can understand out weaknesses and temptations because He was *in all points tempted like as we are, yet without sin.* I believe it is possible this goes further than Jesus' earthly ministry. There is no doubt that Jesus, during His ministry, was tempted as we are and never sinned. The overall message here is that these temptations are not foreign to God; He experienced them Himself. Given that, He understands what we are going through.

I believe many times we might find ourselves considering this as an antiquated message without realizing it. There are temptations and hardships we go through in our modern age on a daily basis that we might be tempted to think God never had to deal with. For example, consider the many temptations that come from our modern technological devices that were not available in the time Jesus walked the earth. We might even take this further and find ourselves believing there are situations we go through that bring about great heartache, pain, and loss that Jesus may not have dealt with.

I propose that God truly does understand, not only because He dealt with the same basic temptations during His earthly ministry, but because He dwells in us. I believe this means He goes through all of our personal experiences with us. This idea goes beyond temptation and weakness; it deals with our hurt, joy, pain, loss, gain, happiness, and tragedy. If God truly dwells in our spirit, and if our spirit is who we actually are as individuals, then God understands us in a way no one else can. When we go through experiences in life, He understands because He is living it too, right there with us. When we go through times of personal triumph, He celebrates with us. When we go through times of tragedy and loss, He cries with us. When we go through times of heartache and despair, He hurts with us. Not only does He do all of these things, but He also comforts us, strengthens us, and encourages us. We are never alone.

Eternal Reality

There is one last thing I want to explore. We know that, as Christians, we have eternal life. We also know that we will all have to die someday. Again, we understand the basics of this; our body dies but our spirit lives on. However, I believe it goes far deeper. The first thing to keep in mind is that time itself is a creation of God. That means God Himself is outside of time. God is also eternal. This means that "eternity" is not just a long expanse of time, or even an infinite amount of time for that matter. If it were, it would mean the inherent quality of God's eternality is something He created outside of Himself that could not have existed without Him creating it. It would be comparable to saying that God is love, yet love did not exist until God created it. It is a paradox. As far as what eternity actually is, the best way I can reconcile it is to think of eternity as more of a place or a state of existence outside of what we recognize as dimensional time.

The reason we can never truly die is because the Spirit of God dwells in our spirit. Our physical body will die, however when that takes place, God brings us beyond the veil into eternity. What that exactly will look like, I can only speculate, however it is something we can all look forward to. The end of the physical life of our natural body is not truly the end; it is merely the beginning of our life in eternity.

Afterword

Written by Perelandra Kilns of Watcher Vault

www.watchervault.com

One of the beautiful qualities about a book like the one you are holding is that it is the product of an earnest and sincere desire to plumb the infinite depths of truth for the benefit of one's fellow man. When Pontius Pilate asked Jesus that question which has captivated the minds of philosophers for millennia, *What is truth?*, he did not realize the utter irony of the question for the very one he asked was the eternal and infinite Truth. As finite beings, Christians being renewed in mind by the saving grace of Truth embodied, it is impossible for us to reach the end of the question and discovery process which is a part of "enjoying Him forever" as His image-bearers.

If the Word of God contains objective truth then it is the light by which any and all questions should be considered. Josh Peck goes by the book as he considers questions and possibilities in *Cherubim Chariots* and his previous publications that bring much food for thought to the minds of readers who are curious about topics that are sometimes considered either taboo or unanswerable by an unprepared church.

When one espouses this high view of Scripture all things begin to come into focus. Science, history, world religion, myth and legend, philosophy, culture: all of these broad subjects are navigable by the light of scripture and we are able to consider the pieces of the puzzle of this fallen world on a strong foundation. Just as a two-dimensional Flatlander might be disbelieved by his skeptical fellows in his descriptions of intelligent three-dimensional beings, so might it also be difficult for three-dimensional human beings to consider a higher dimensional intelligence as actually in existence - yet the scriptures make it plain. We do not even have to guess at that reality because it is stated for us in Ephesians 6:12:

"For we do not wrestle against flesh and blood, but against the rulers, against the authorities, against the cosmic powers over this present darkness, against the spiritual forces of evil in the heavenly places."

Humanity has "wrestled against" these higher-dimensional intelligences since the fall of man in the perfect garden, Eden. These intelligences take seriously their role to steal away man's love of goodness, truth, and beauty in Christ and replace it with another idea; a lie. They have one ultimate goal: to take humanity down with them, forever separated from our Creator. As I write this, History Channel's *Ancient Aliens* Facebook fan page has 1,208,487 likes. This television show presents an alternative view of the above mentioned spiritual forces going so far as to suggest that they are our creators and behind many various events in history. In a sense, they are not so far off the mark. These forces do indeed seek to influence history but they are not our creators nor our friends.

Thankfully, *Cherubim Chariots* seeks to provide thoughtful, biblically researched possibilities to the inner workings and agenda of an historical phenomenon that in recent times has piqued the mainstream attention of the world - that of the UFO and the other-worldly visitor.

Perelandra Kilns

January 12, 2015

33rd Parallel North

www.WatcherVault.com

John 18: 36-38

Jesus answered, "My kingdom is not of this world. If My kingdom were of this world, then My servants would be fighting so that I would not be handed over to the Jews; but as it is, My kingdom is not of this realm." Therefore Pilate said to Him, "So You are a king?" Jesus answered, "You say correctly that I am a king. For this I have been born, and for this I have come into the world, to testify to the truth. Everyone who is of the truth hears My voice." Pilate said to Him,

"What is truth?"

About the Author

Josh Peck is a Christian author and biblical researcher. He is the author of *Quantum Creation: Does the Supernatural Lurk in the Fourth Dimension?* and *Disclosure: Unveiling Our Role in the Secret War of the Ancients.* He works toward waking up the Church to the reality of the Bible, separating biblical truth from Church tradition when necessary, and providing the solid, raw, and uncut truth of God's Word to any and all who are interested. He is the founder of Ministudy Ministry, the goal of which is to provide short, personal, and inexpensive study materials for the average at-home Bible reader, study group, and church. Josh Peck also hosts an internet show entitled The Sharpening, which features regular guests and Bible study covering a wide range of topics. All past and upcoming episodes of The Sharpening can be found at www.youtube.com/joshpeckdisclosure. For more information about Josh Peck, Ministudy Ministry, and The Sharpening, visit www.ministudyministry.com.

Other Titles by Josh Peck

Available at www.MinistudyMinistry.com

QUANTUM CREATION

Does the Supernatural Lurk in the Fourth Dimension?

Foreword by S. Douglas Woodward

Includes Interviews with: Kenneth Johnson - Original Creator of V and Alien Nation, Dr. Ronald Mallett - Professor and Theoretical Physicist, Dr. Ken Johnson - Biblical Researcher and Author

Is there a way for science and religion to complement one another? Does quantum physics have any place in the Bible? Do biblical interpretations have any use in explaining scientific observations? Is quantum physics unknowable to religious minds? Must a scientific mind also be void of religion? Is there an unseen world that exists all around us? Do things like strings, branes, multiple dimensions, parallel universes, time warps, quantum entanglement, and extradimensional beings have any place in biblical descriptions of God's creation?

These questions and more are addressed in Quantum Creation. For the first time ever, the study of quantum physics is made available to the religious mind while explaining theological implications. Even better yet, the information is presented in a way anybody can understand.

Learn just how perfectly compatible science and religion can be and why it seems they are always at odds. Discover what really makes up everything in existence as reality itself is examined at a quantum level. Find out if things like time travel are scientifically and biblically possible. What is presented in Quantum Creation is the answer to how science and religion really can go hand in hand. Finally, a way to look at the strange and fascinating world of quantum physics from a biblical perspective is here.

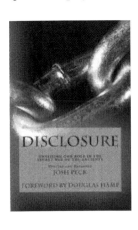

DISCLOSURE - UPDATED AND EXPANDED

Unveiling Our Role in the Secret War of the Ancients

Updated and Expanded

Foreword by Douglas Hamp

There is a war against humanity that has been raging for nearly six thousand years. The Great Commander, Jesus Christ, has set up

His Church to fight the enemy. The problem is the enemy has convinced the Church that the war does not exist.

Many Christians today are unknowingly being hidden away from true Bible prophecy. Disclosure answers this problem by guiding a Christian through even the most traditional beliefs to the exciting world of God's promises and prophecy, including topics such as the Nephilim and the green horse of Revelation. There has never been a more important time in history for the Church to be informed. The enemy is setting the stage for the greatest deception the world has ever seen. Disclosure sorts out truth from tradition and digs out the hidden prophecies that God has left for us in His Word.

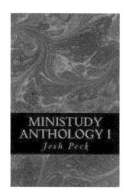

MINISTUDY ANTHOLOGY I

Welcome to the first collection of Ministudy Books by author Josh Peck! Included are the first five Ministudy books ever produced by Ministudy Ministry. You will never again find a collection that offers so much biblical information that can lead you to a closer relationship with God and His Son Jesus Christ.

Titles include: The Four Degrees of Baptism, Spiritual Warfare against the Satanic Government, The Day of the Lord,

Sorting out the Resurrection and Ascensions of Christ, and What Loving God Really Means (previously unreleased title).

Plus extra bonus writings by Josh Peck!

PECK'S HARMONY OF THE GOSPELS

A Chronological Gospel Harmony from the King James Version Bible

Get ready to experience the Gospels like never before! The idea behind this Gospel Harmony is to blend the four Gospels into a single, coherent, and chronological narrative. This provides a clearer picture and appreciation for the life of Jesus; what He did, when He did it, and what it means for all of us today. This Gospel Harmony is a wonderful tool for personal study and enjoyment of the first four books of the New Testament taken from the King James Version of the Holy Bible.

In the past, there have been many wonderful attempts at harmonizing the four Gospels. There are many features of this Gospel Harmony that are not found in any other:

- Gospels separated by font-emphasis instead of parallel columns for a great reading experience (Matthew in regular text, Mark in underlined text, Luke in italic text, and John in bold text);

- Chronological order;
- Verse number included for every verse;
- Chapter and verse number references for every time the Gospel or section changes;
- A Table of Contents of large sections in the front of the book;
- A Table of Contents of small sections in the back of the book;

And much more!

*   *   *

Visit www.MinistudyMinistry.com for a complete list of books and eBooks available by Josh Peck.

Contributing Authors

Mark A. Flynn

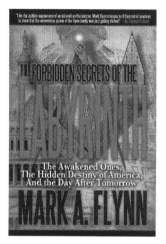

Mark Flynn is the author of *Forbidden Secrets of the Labyrinth: The Awakened Ones, the Hidden Destiny of America, and the Day After Tomorrow.* Visit www.MarkAFlynn.com for more information on Mark, his work, and his ministry.

Cris Putnam

Cris Putnam is the author of *The Supernatural Worldview.* Visit www.SupernaturalWorldview.com and www.LogosApologia.org for more information on Cris, his work, and his ministry.

Sharon K. Gilbert

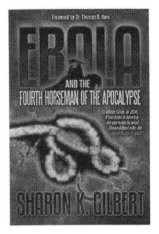

Sharon Gilbert is the author of *Ebola and the Fourth Horseman of the Apocalypse*. Visit www.SharonKGilbert.com for more information on Sharon, her work, and her ministry.

S. Douglas Woodward

Doug Woodward is author of *Blood Moons: Biblical Signs of the Coming Apocalypse*. Visit www.Faith-Happens.com for more information on Doug, his work, and his ministry.

Perelandra Kilns

 Perelandra Kilns maintains the Watcher Vault website, a repository for the work and research of the original "watcher", David Flynn. Visit www.WatcherVault.com for more information on Perelandra, her work, and her ministry.

Made in the USA
Charleston, SC
10 February 2015